CULTURA IN
2.° ANO

BY
ME

CULTURA IN
2.º ANO

Welcome back Katie and Ben		Page 4	An introduction to the course characters
Welcome back Sam and Amy		Page 5	An introduction to the course characters
1	**How my body works**	Page 6	**STORY** Party games
2	**Look after yourself**	Page 20	**STORY** Be careful!
3	**The animal kingdom**	Page 34	**STORY** Living and non living things
4	**Music land**	Page 48	**DISCOVER** • La, si and high do • The world of music
5	**The Solar System**	Page 58	**STORY** Which planet?
6	**Air and water**	Page 70	**STORY** Measuring the weather
	Picture dictionary	Page 84	Key vocabulary for all six units

		LET'S INVESTIGATE	MAKE A DIFFERENCE	LET'S REMEMBER
CONTENT • Our five senses • We breathe oxygen • We eat food • Our body has bones	• Our body has muscles • Our body has joints • We grow and change	How our muscles work	Look after your body	Review of Unit 1
CONTENT • Our body needs protection • A balanced diet • Healthy meals • Exercise	• Healthy habits • We are different • Be a good friend	Digestion	Look after your teeth	Review of Unit 2
CONTENT • Vertebrates and invertebrates • Mammals • Birds	• Reptiles and amphibians • Fish • Arthropods • Molluscs	What animals eat	Be a scientist	Review of Unit 3
LISTEN AND PLAY • Metre • Percussion in a symphony orchestra		**SING** Different voices	**CREATE** Form a symphony orchestra	Review of Unit 4
CONTENT • The planets • The planets move around the Sun	• The Moon moves around the Earth • Day and night • Seasons and years	The Sun, Earth and Moon	Look after your planet	Review of Unit 5
CONTENT • Wind and clouds • Precipitation • What is the weather like today?	• What is air? • What is water? • The water cycle • Water around us	Make a weather vane	Saving energy	Review of Unit 6

Welcome back Katie and Ben

1) 🔊 Listen and point. Find Katie and Ben.

2) ✏️ What do you need at school? Tick.

pencil   textbook   recorder

rubber   sweets   notebook

4   four

Welcome back Sam and Amy

1. 🔊 Listen and point. Find Sam and Amy.

2. 🔊 🖍 Listen and circle. Use the code.

⭕ Sam   ⭕ Amy

five 5

1 How my body works

1. Name three things you can eat.
2. Circle five things you can hear.
3. Who is not feeling well?
4. Listen and number the things in the order you hear them.
5. Sing the song and do the actions!

Party games

1 🔊 **Listen, look and point.**

2 🔊 **Listen and draw lines.**

see

hear

smell

taste

touch

8   eight

Our five senses

Our **eyes**, **ears**, **nose**, **tongue** and **skin** collect information and send it to our **brain**. Our brain helps us to understand the world around us. Which sense is Katie using?

1 Which sense are they using? Write.

2 What do we see, hear, smell, taste and touch? Draw.

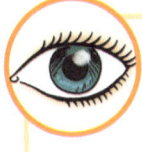  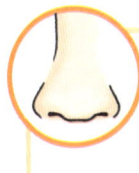

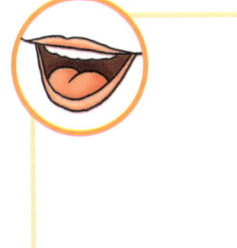 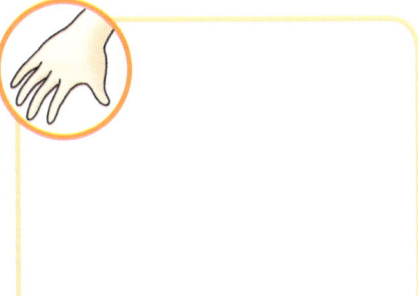

We breathe oxygen

Our body needs **oxygen**. Oxygen comes from the air we breathe into our **lungs**. Our **heart** pumps the oxygen around the rest of our body in our **blood**. Exercise keeps our lungs and heart healthy. What is Katie doing?

1 Listen and circle.

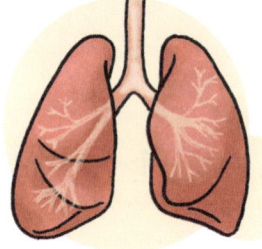   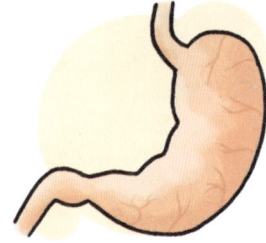   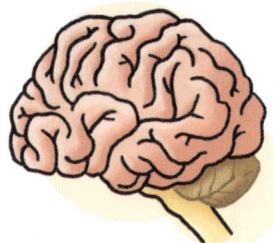   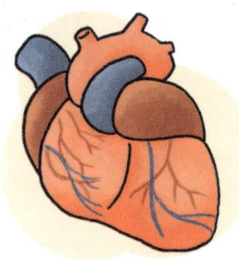

lungs   stomach   brain   heart

2 Circle the correct answer.

respiration   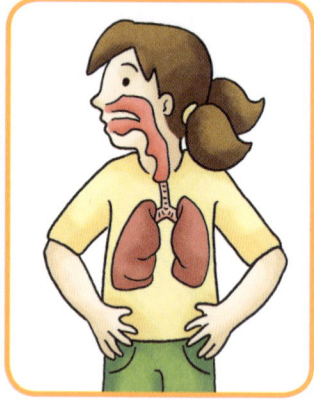   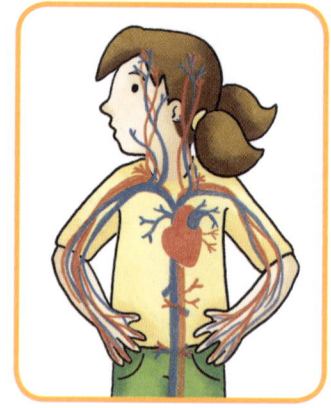   respiration

circulation   circulation

3 What keeps our lungs and heart healthy? Tick.

10 ten

We eat food

Our body needs food to grow, be active and stay healthy. Our **digestive system** breaks down the food and absorbs its **nutrients**. Nutrients travel to the rest of our body in our **bloodstream**. What is Ben eating?

1 Listen to the *Digestion* chant. Number.

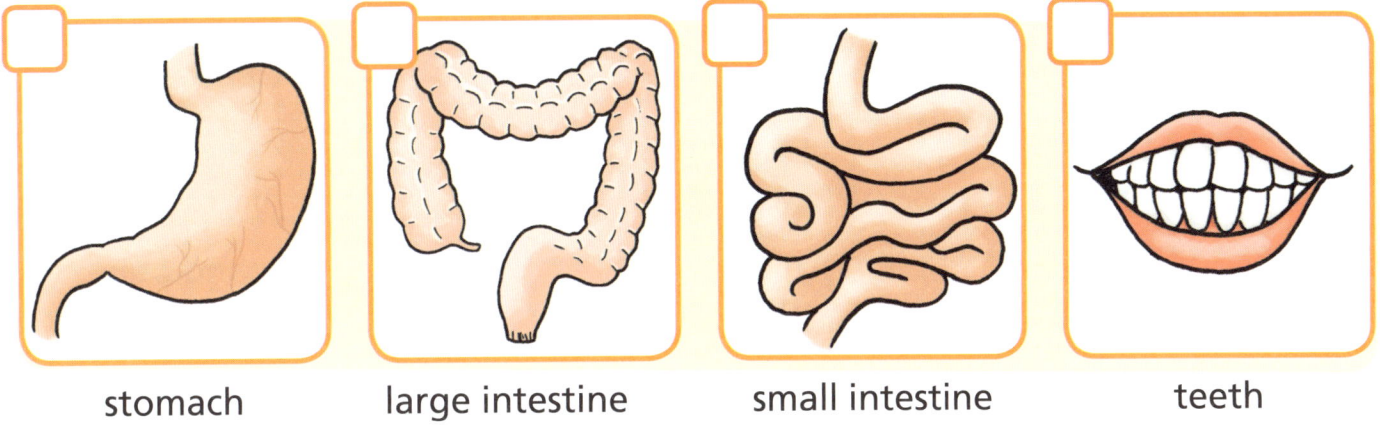

stomach   large intestine   small intestine   teeth

2 Listen again. Label the picture then draw the route of the food.

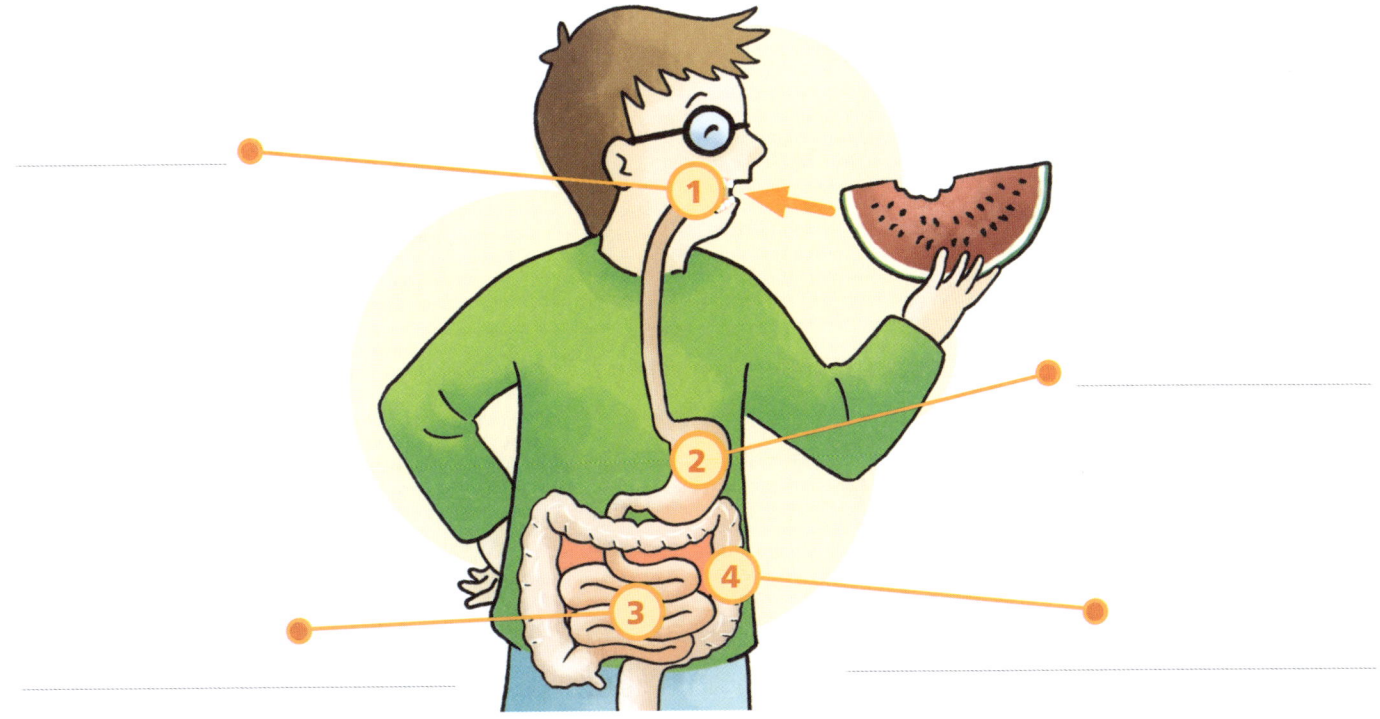

Our body has bones

Our **skeleton** is made up of many bones. It supports our body. As we grow, our bones grow too. Our skeleton protects organs such as our **brain**, **heart** and **lungs**. Which of Ben's bones can you see?

1 Listen to the *Connected bones* chant. Point.

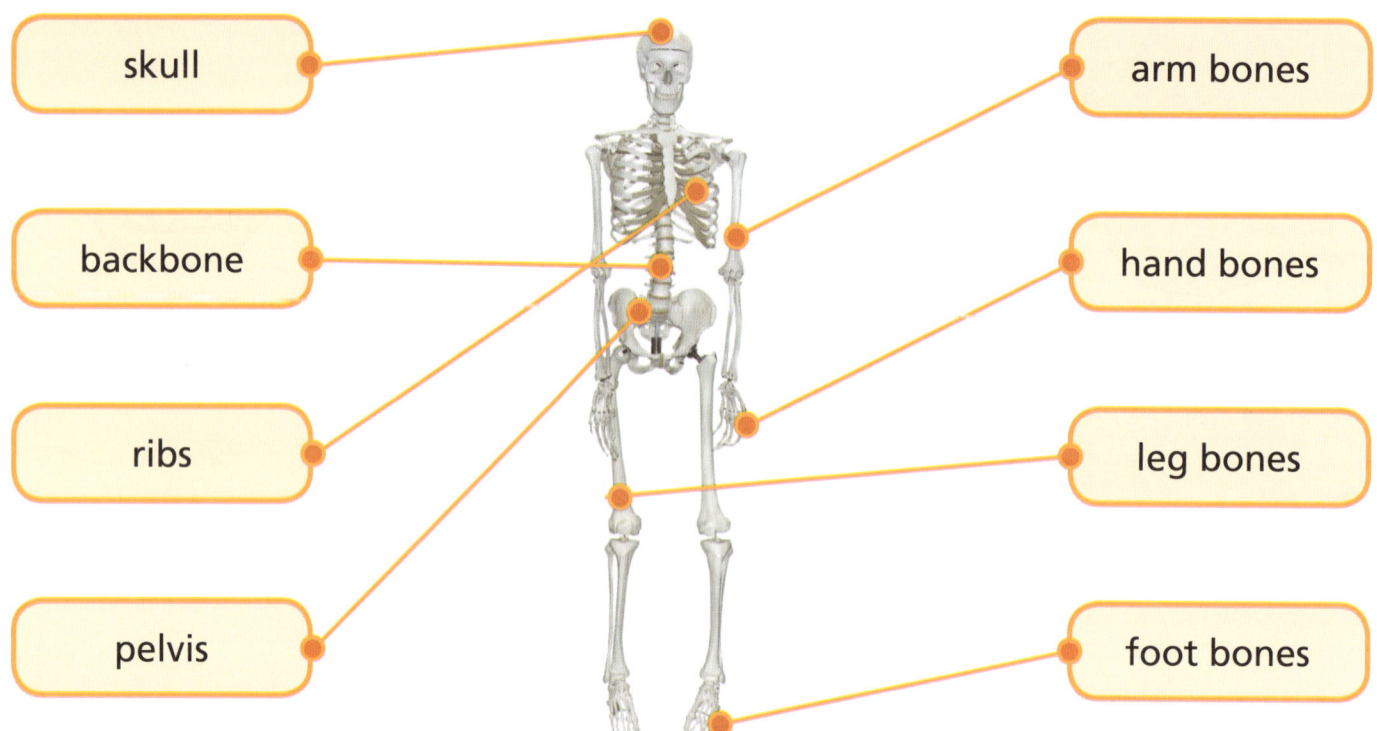

- skull
- backbone
- ribs
- pelvis
- arm bones
- hand bones
- leg bones
- foot bones

2 Find the stickers.

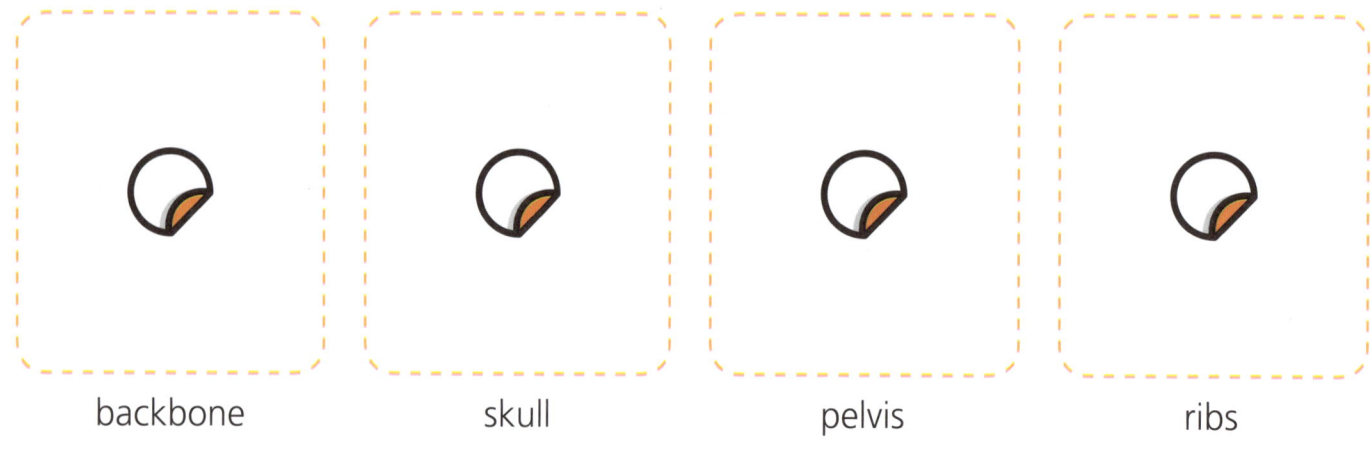

backbone · skull · pelvis · ribs

12 twelve

Our body has muscles

Muscles help move our bones. All our bones have muscles connected to them. Muscles work in pairs to pull the bones. Which muscle is Katie touching?

1 🔊 Look and listen. Feel your muscles.

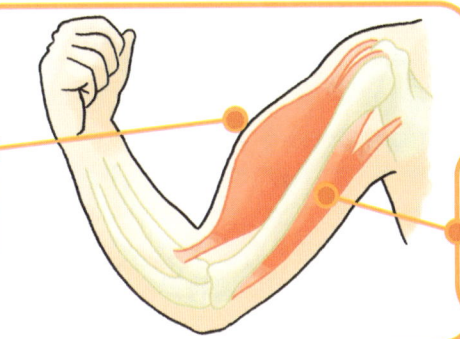

Our **biceps** muscle contracts (gets shorter and fatter) and **pulls up** our arm.

Our **triceps** muscle relaxes (gets longer and thinner).

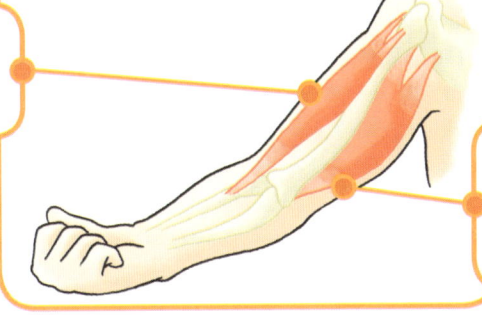

Our **biceps** muscle relaxes.

Our **triceps** muscle contracts and **pulls down** our arm.

2 🔊 ✏️ Listen to how our arm muscles help us. Number.

catch

carry

pick up

hold

thirteen **13**

Our body has joints

1 Label the joints.

- neck
- wrist
- finger
- ankle
- toe

- jaw
- shoulder
- elbow
- hip
- knee

2   Draw what is missing. Circle the joints.

A **joint** is the place where two or more bones come together. Our **skeleton** bends and moves at the joints with help from our **muscles**. Which joints are helping Ben ride his bicycle?

14 fourteen

We grow and change

We all grow and change. Women can have **babies**. Babies become **children**. Children become **adolescents** (teenagers). Adolescents become **adults**. How does Ben change?

1 🔊 ✏️ Listen and number. Trace.

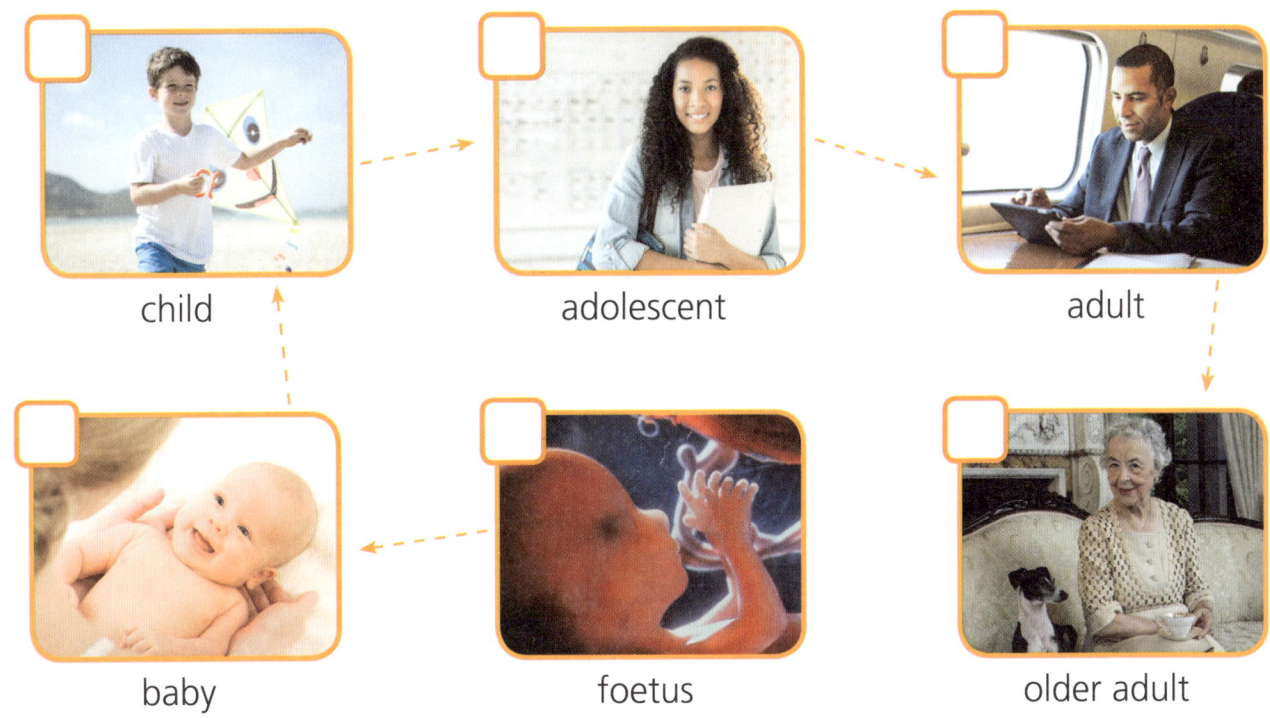

child — adolescent — adult

baby — foetus — older adult

2 🎨 How do you change? Draw.

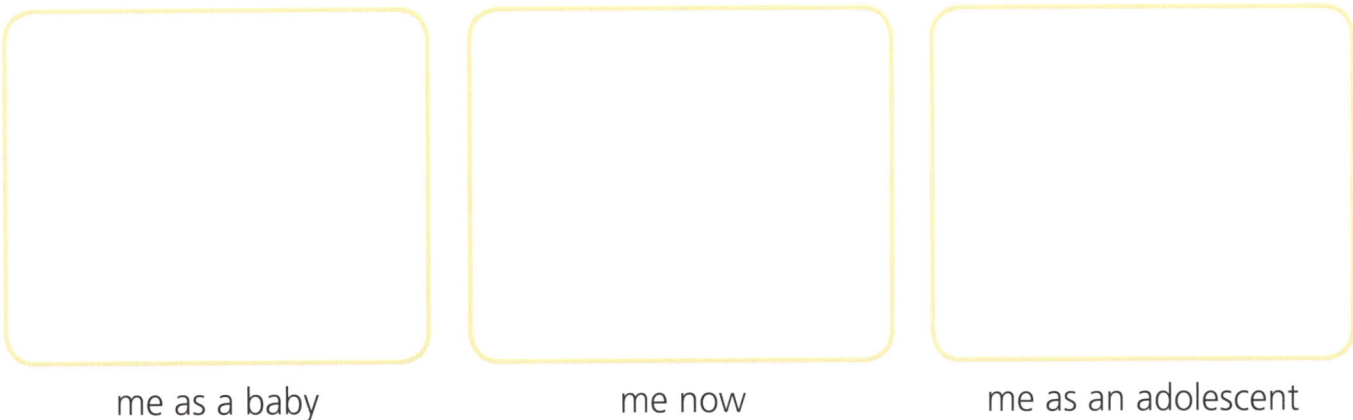

me as a baby — me now — me as an adolescent

fifteen **15**

LET'S INVESTIGATE: How our muscles work

Idea:
A muscle contracts and relaxes.

Test:

Step 1
Colour and cut out a paper model of a biceps muscle.

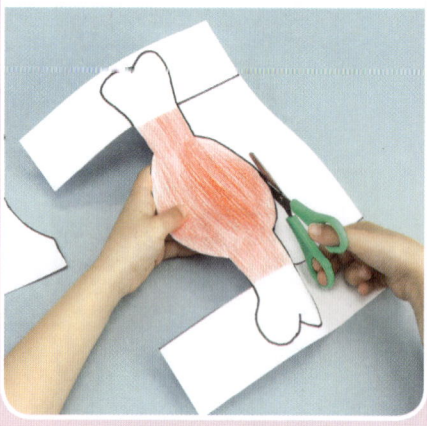

Step 2
Attach it to your arm with tape.

Step 3
Bend and straighten your arm.

1 Read and put a tick or a cross.

☐ When I bend my arm, the biceps muscle gets shorter and fatter.

☐ When I straighten my arm, the biceps muscle gets longer and thinner.

☐ The biceps muscle is located in the torso.

What is the name of the muscle that works with the biceps muscle?

MAKE A DIFFERENCE: Look after your body

1 🔊 🎨 Who is looking after their bones and muscles? Listen and colour **green**.

2 👥 Make a *Look after your body* poster.

1 Draw or cut out pictures.

2 Draw and cut out bones and muscles.

3 Stick your pictures on the bones and muscles. Write your advice.

seventeen **17**

Let's remember

1. Write.

teeth   lungs   stomach   heart

We breathe with our _____.

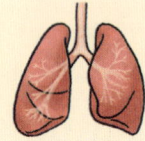

Our _____ pumps blood around our body.

Our _____ chew food.

Our _____ digests food.

2. Complete the crossword.

3 Read and circle.

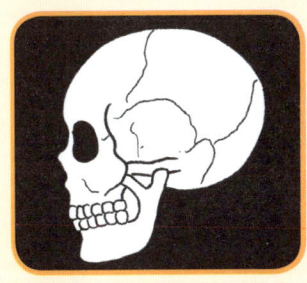 This is my **skull / pelvis**.

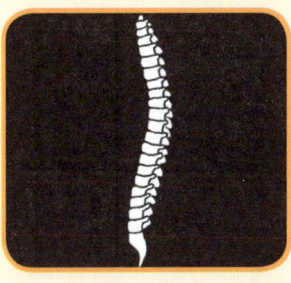 This is my **arm bone / backbone**.

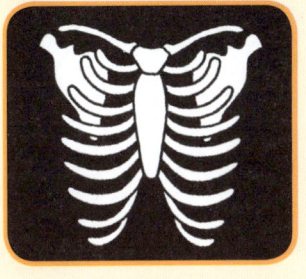 These are my **finger bones / ribs**.

 This is my **foot bone / pelvis**.

4 Write.

child   adolescent   adult   baby

 →  →  →

_____   _____   _____   _____

Name the organs we use to breathe and eat.

Locate some bones in my body.

Explain why we have muscles.

Explain how we grow and change.

Well done! Choose a sticker.

2 Look after yourself

1. How many different activities can you see?
2. Circle two children working together.
3. Who is not happy? Who is not behaving properly?
4. Listen and draw the missing body parts. Write.

arms knees hips

ankles

5. Sing the song and do the actions!

Be careful!

1 🔊 Listen, look and point.

2 ➕ ✏️ Look and read. Write *yes* or *no*.

   It protects your head.   _____

   They protect your feet.   _____

   They protect your knees.   _____

22 twenty-two

Our body needs protection

We can **prevent accidents**. We need to **be alert**, **protect** our bodies and **wear** the correct clothes when we do exercise. Why is Katie putting on these shoes?

1 Listen to the advice and number the children. Who is being careful?

2 Match.

Wear the correct protection.

Be alert and use your senses.

Don't do dangerous activities.

twenty-three **23**

A balanced diet

We categorise food into **food groups**. The foods in each food group help our bodies in different ways. A **balanced diet** means we eat a variety of healthy food. We also need to drink plenty of **water** every day. Is Ben drinking a healthy drink?

1 🔊 ✏️ Listen and look. Tick the things the food groups give us.

1. carbohydrates
   - ☐ help us grow
   - ☐ give us energy

2. fats
   - ☐ help us grow
   - ☐ give us energy

3. proteins
   - ☐ help us grow
   - ☐ give us energy

4. dairy products
   - ☐ are good for our bones and teeth
   - ☐ give us energy

5. fruit and vegetables
   - ☐ keep us healthy
   - ☐ help us grow

Healthy meals

We have three main **meals** a day: **breakfast**, **lunch** and **dinner**. If we are hungry between meals, we can have one or two **snacks**. Choose healthy snacks that are not **sugary**. Is Katie eating a healthy snack?

1 Listen and look. Circle the lunch the girl is describing.

2 Draw your school snack today and your favourite school snack. Tick the box.

healthy ☐   unhealthy ☐   healthy ☐   unhealthy ☐

| my snack today | my favourite snack |

twenty-five **25**

Exercise

We need to do some **physical exercise** every day. Exercise makes our bones and muscles **strong**, and it makes us feel good and **relaxed**. What is Ben doing? Do you do this exercise?

1 What exercise do you do? Circle.

2 Listen to the *Exercise* chant. Number.

Healthy habits

It is important to look after your body and **keep clean**. **Sleep** is also very important. On school nights, we should go to bed early. What time does Katie go to bed?

1 Read and find the stickers.

1. I wash my hands with soap and water before I eat.
2. I sleep well at night.
3. I brush my teeth two or three times a day.

2 Complete the healthy habits table about you. Add ticks.

I eat	healthy snacks ☐	three main meals ☐	lots of sweets ☐
At night, I sleep	6 hours ☐	8 hours ☐	at least 10 hours ☐
I brush my teeth	once a day ☐	twice a day ☐	three times a day ☐
I exercise	every day ☐	a few times a week ☐	once a month ☐
I wash my hands	with water ☐	with soap and water ☐	before I eat ☐

twenty-seven 27

We are different

1 🔊 **Listen and say the name.**

Katie   Sally   Sara   Ben   Dan   Alex

2 🔊 ✏️ **Listen and read. Match.**

I have a big family.

I have a small family.

I like playing football.

I like doing karate.

I can play the violin.

I can speak English.

○ We are all **different**. Our bodies and faces are different. We like different things and we can do different activities. How are Katie and Ben different?

28 twenty-eight

Be a good friend

Good friends **help** you, **listen** to you and **share** their things with you. Good friends play together and **play nicely**. Good friends have fun together. Is Katie a good friend?

1 🔊 ✏️ Look and listen. Who is a good friend? Tick.

LET'S INVESTIGATE: Digestion

Idea: Our teeth and stomach break down food.

Test:

Step 1
Crush two of the sweets.

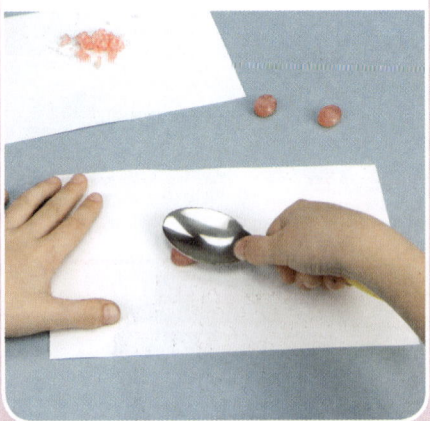

Step 2
Put one whole sweet in water and one in vinegar.

Step 3
Put one crushed sweet in water and one in vinegar.

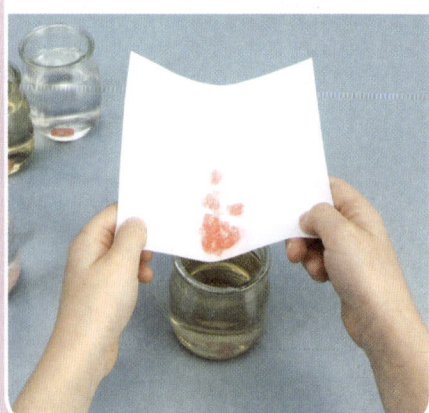

1 Read and put a tick or a cross.

☐ The whole sweets dissolve faster.

☐ The crushed sweet in vinegar dissolves faster.

☐ The crushed sweet in water dissolves faster.

What happens to food when we eat it?

MAKE A DIFFERENCE: Look after your teeth

1 🔊 ✏️ Listen and tick the good advice.

Brush your teeth twice a day.

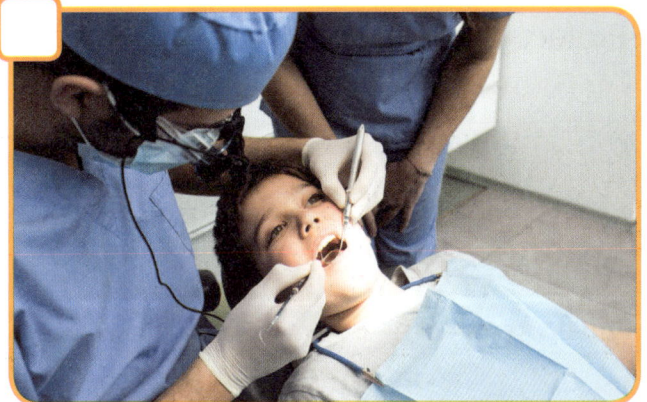
Visit the dentist regularly.

Eat lots of sweets.

Eat healthy food.

2 👥 Look after your teeth. Make a mini book.

❶ Give your book a title.
❷ Draw and write about teeth.
❸ Leave your mini book in the library for other pupils to read!

Let's remember

1 ✏️ **Read and number the photos.**

① Protect your body.　② Be alert.　③ Don't do dangerous activities.

2 ✏️ **Match the food to the correct group.**

　　　　　　　fruit and vegetables

　　　　　　　carbohydrates

　　　　　　　dairy products

　　　　　　　proteins

3. Interview two friends. Put a tick or a cross.

	My friend _____	My friend _____
Do you eat healthy food every day?		
Do you drink lots of water every day?		
Do you exercise every day?		
Do you sleep well every night?		
Do you wash every day?		
Do you brush your teeth two or three times a day?		

4. Look and say what you see.

	😐	🙂	😀
Know how to be safe and healthy.			
Know the different food groups.			
Know how to look after my body and keep clean.			
Know how to be a good friend.			

Well done! Choose a sticker.

thirty-three 33

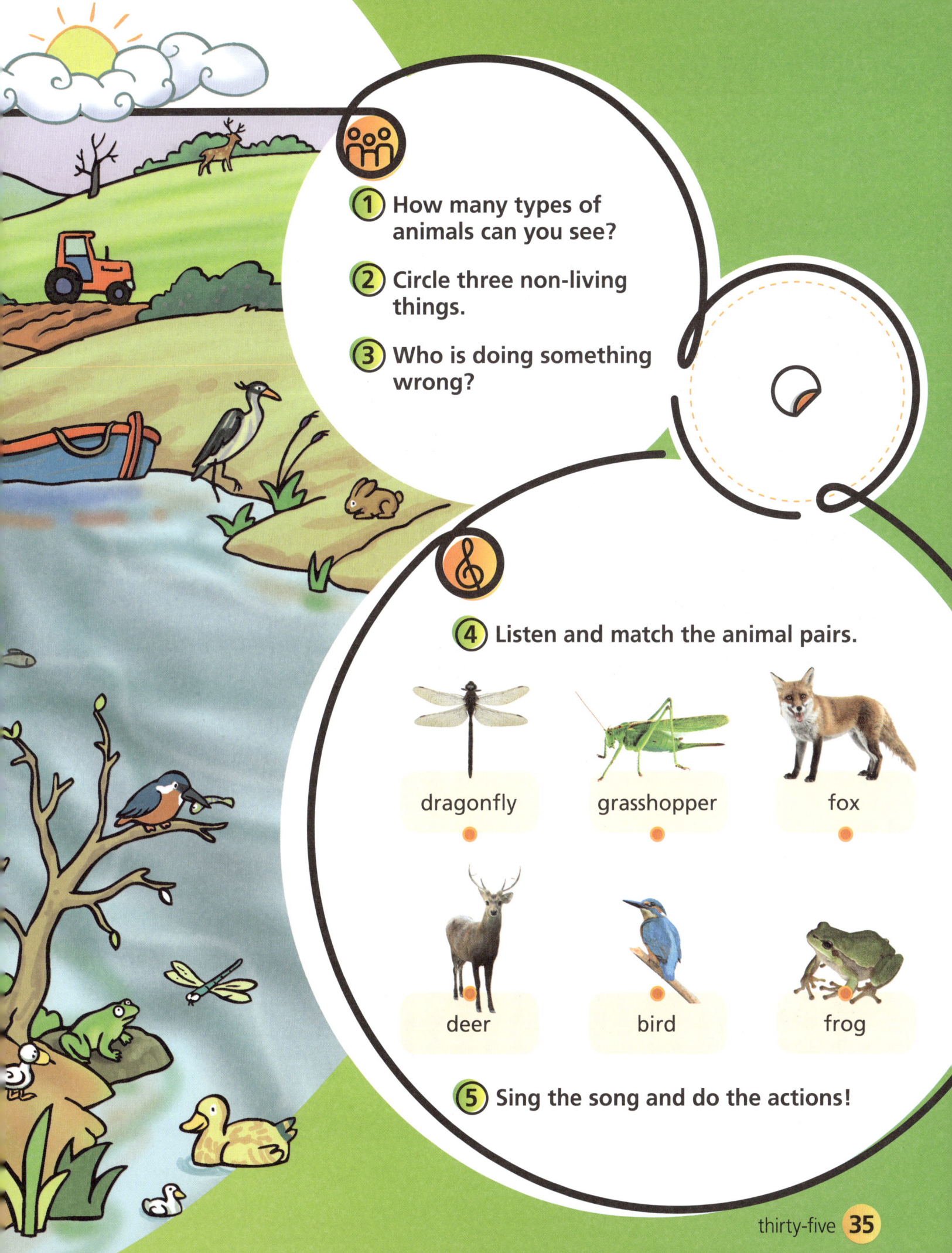

1. How many types of animals can you see?
2. Circle three non-living things.
3. Who is doing something wrong?

4. Listen and match the animal pairs.

dragonfly   grasshopper   fox

deer   bird   frog

5. Sing the song and do the actions!

thirty-five 35

Living and non-living things

1 🔊 Listen, look and point.

2 ➕ 🔊 📖 Listen and tick the correct information.

All living things …

reproduce   can fly   die   grow

Vertebrates and invertebrates

The animal kingdom is divided into two groups: **vertebrates** and **invertebrates**. Vertebrates have a backbone and invertebrates do not. Which group do we belong to?

1 Look at the skeletons. Write the animal.

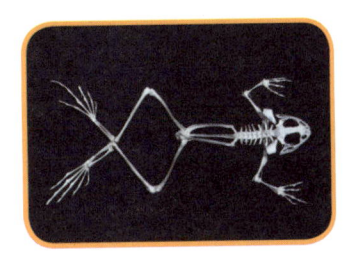

2 Listen and complete the classification diagram.

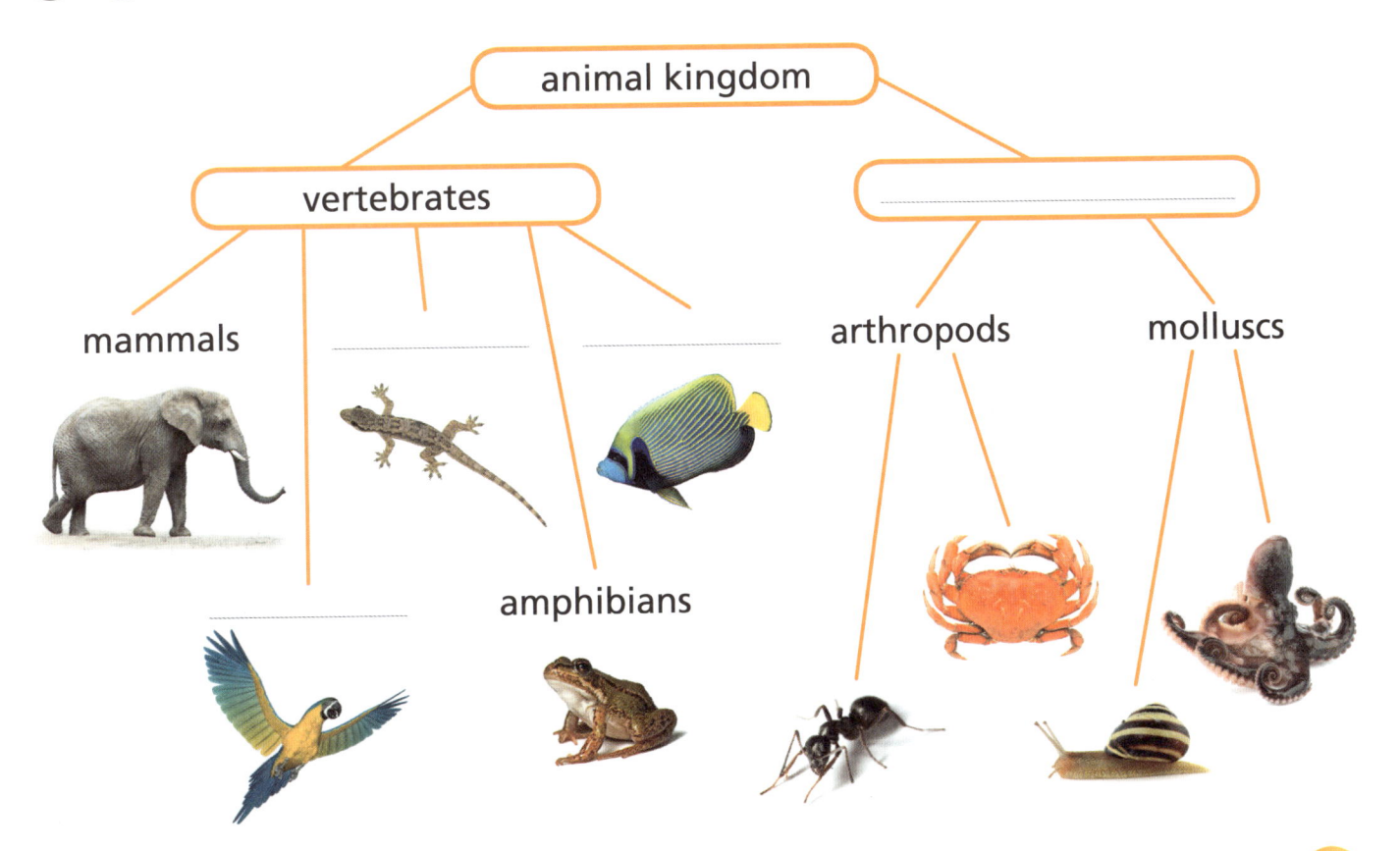

- animal kingdom
  - vertebrates
    - mammals
    - amphibians
    - arthropods
    - molluscs

thirty-seven 37

Mammals

1 🔊 ✏️ Listen and number two examples.

Mammals …

1. … have hair or fur.
2. … are viviparous and have live babies who drink milk.
3. … are herbivores, carnivores or omnivores.
4. … live in different habitats.
5. … move in different ways.

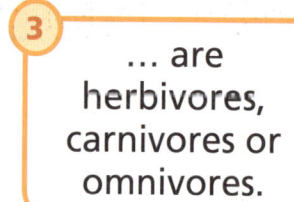

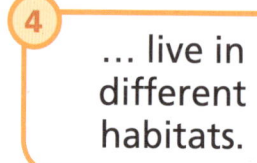

> Mammals are **viviparous**. They have **hair** or **fur**. They can be **herbivores**, **carnivores** or **omnivores**. Mammals live in different **habitats** and can **move** in different ways. What mammal is Ben watching?

Birds

1 🔊 ✏️ **Listen and write.**

| feathers | eggs | wings | beak | tail |

2 ✏️ **What do birds eat? Circle the food.**

○ **Birds** have **feathers**, **wings**, two legs and a **beak**. Birds are **oviparous**. They lay eggs with hard shells. They live in different habitats. Most birds can fly. What type of bird is Katie feeding? Can it fly?

thirty-nine 39

Reptiles and amphibians

1 🔊 ✏️ **Listen and trace the correct arrows.**

reptiles — amphibians

- They live on land and in water.
- They have soft, moist skin.
- They have dry skin and scales.
- They lay hard eggs on land.
- They lay soft eggs in water.
- They breathe with lungs.
- They breathe with gills and later with lungs.

2 🎼 ✏️ **Listen to the *What am I?* chant. Number. Are they reptiles or amphibians?**

> Reptiles lay **hard eggs** on land. They breathe with **lungs** and have **scales**. Amphibians lay **soft eggs** in water. At first they breathe with **gills**, then develop **lungs** when they are adults. They have **moist skin**. What is Katie holding?

40 forty

Fish

Fish have **scales** and **fins**. They breathe with **gills**. They live in rivers, lakes and oceans. They lay **soft eggs** in water. Fish eat plankton, insects, other fish and water plants. Where is Ben?

1 Draw the missing parts. Colour and label.

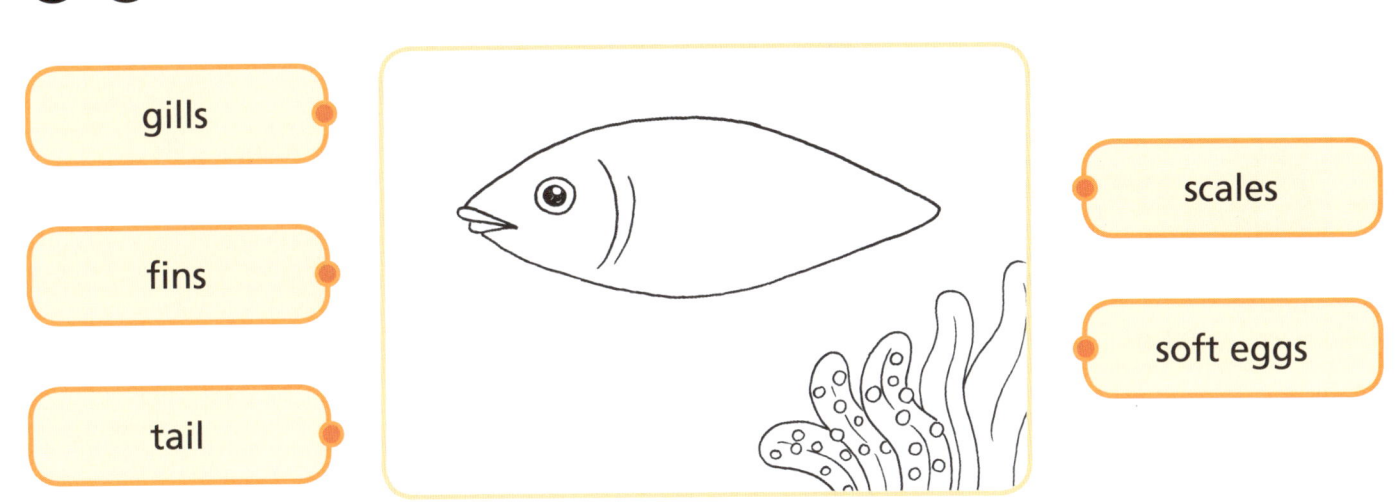

- gills
- fins
- tail
- scales
- soft eggs

2 Which two are not fish? Listen and put a cross.

shark   clownfish   dolphin

trout   whale   swordfish

forty-one 41

Arthropods

Arthropods are invertebrates. They have a **segmented body** and limbs with **joints**. Many have **antennae**. They have external armour that protects their bodies called an **exoskeleton**. What is Katie looking at?

1 Read. Find the stickers.

| thin exoskeleton | limbs with joints | segmented body | thick exoskeleton |

2 Write one name for each description.

1. It has six legs.
2. It has two body segments.
3. It has lots of body segments.
4. It has a thick exoskeleton.
5. It has wings.
6. It has three body segments.

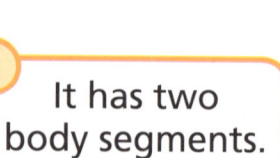

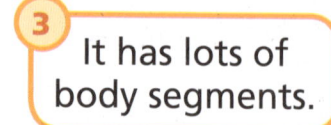

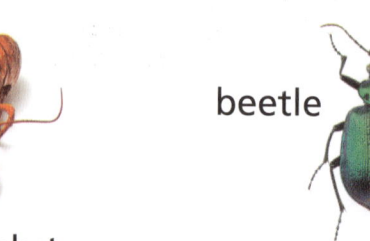

spider

butterfly

lobster

beetle

centipede

42 forty-two

Molluscs

Molluscs are invertebrates. They have a **soft body** and some have a **shell**. Many have **tentacles**. They live in water or moist places. What is in Ben's salad?

1 How many molluscs can you find? Write the number.

- snail ☐
- slug ☐
- mussel ☐ 
- limpet ☐ 
- squid ☐ 

2 Look and label.

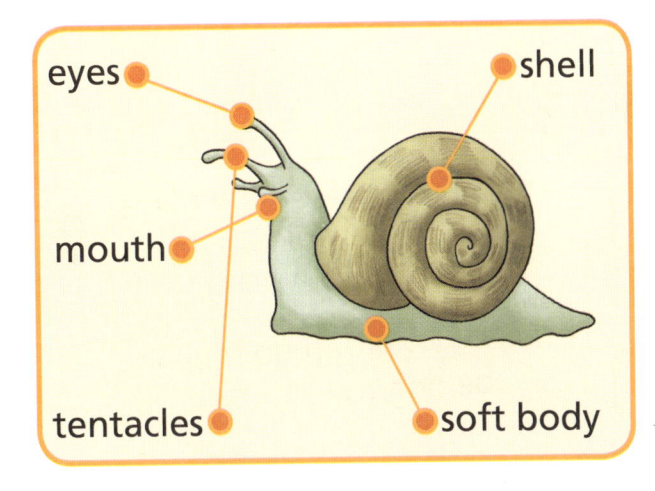

- eyes
- shell
- mouth
- tentacles
- soft body

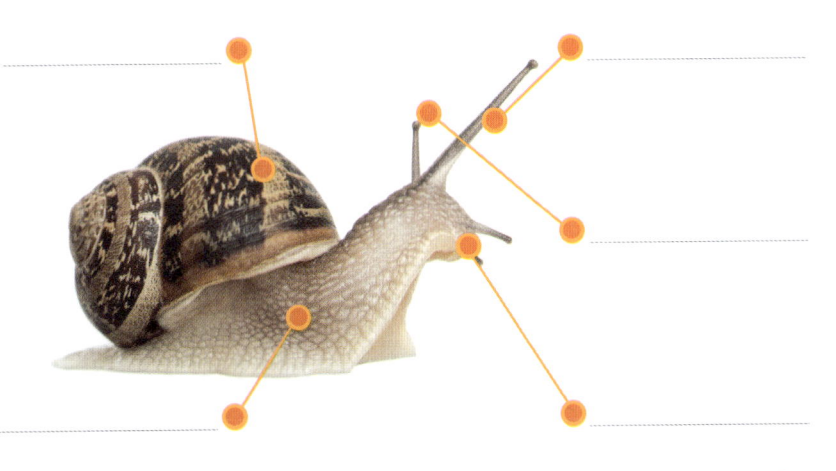

forty-three **43**

LET'S INVESTIGATE: What animals eat

Idea: We can classify animals by what they eat.

Test:

Step 1
Draw a simple diagram with the three groups.

Step 2
Cut out or draw pictures of different animals.

Step 3
Classify and stick the animals in the correct group.

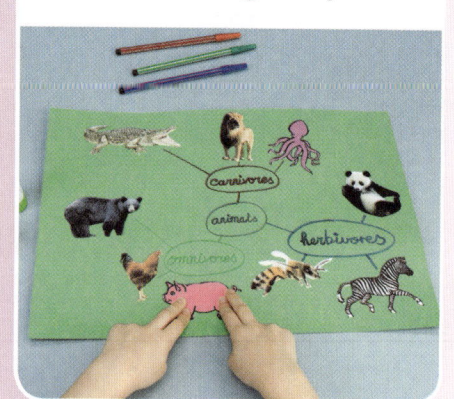

1 ✏️ **Count and write.**

How many invertebrates are there on your poster? ☐

How many carnivores on your poster eat fish? ☐

How many carnivores on your poster eat insects? ☐

Can you spell the names of all the animals on your poster?

What group do humans belong to?

MAKE A DIFFERENCE: Be a scientist

1 🔊 ✏️ Listen and tick what scientists do.

Scientists study and observe.

Scientists classify information.

Scientists paint very well.

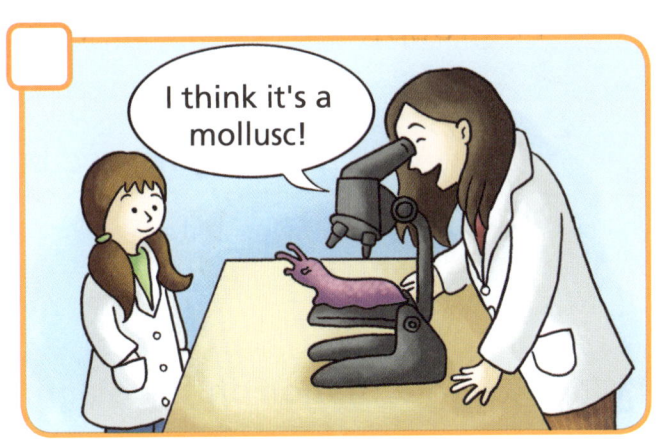

I think it's a mollusc!

Scientists share their ideas.

2 👥 Make a classification poster.

❶ Copy the template.
❷ Write your questions.
❸ Find or draw animal pictures. Stick them on your poster.

forty-five **45**

Let's remember

1 ✏️ Read and circle.

1. It is **viviparous / oviparous**.

2. It is **a carnivore / a herbivore**.

3. It is **a vertebrate / an invertebrate**.

4. It lives **on land / in water**.

5. It has **a segmented body / a soft body**.

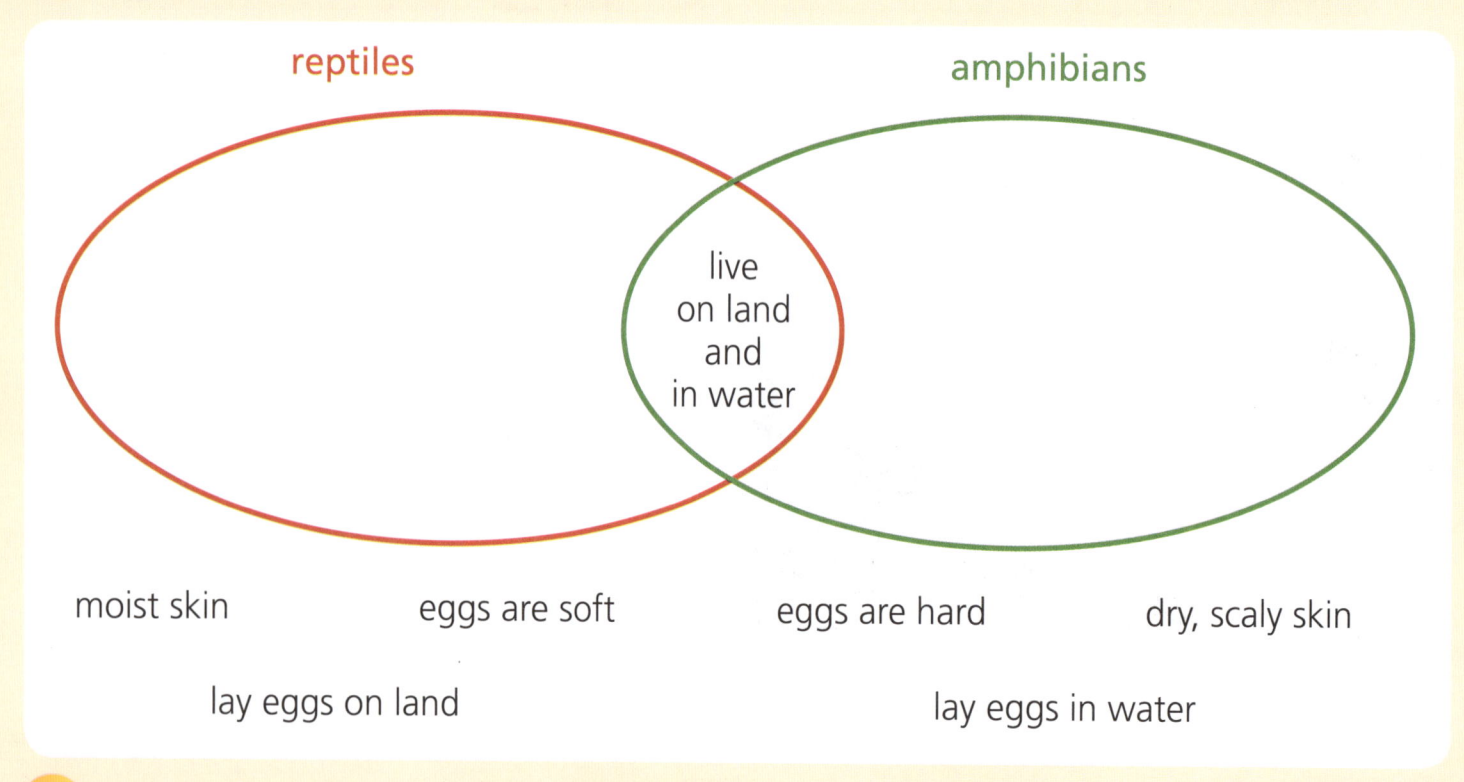

2 ✏️ Write the information on the diagram.

reptiles — amphibians

live on land and in water

moist skin   eggs are soft   eggs are hard   dry, scaly skin

lay eggs on land   lay eggs in water

3 🔊 ✏️ Listen and number. What do the animals have in common?

☐ crocodile   ☐ penguin   ☐ shark   ☐ squid

4 ✏️ How many arthropods can you find?

```
s c o r p i o n c f
b e b e e t l e r d
u n g f f m o p a r
t t a w w z s e b a
t i s a d a p p y g
e p r s t h i r i o
r e g p e m d a d n
f d e a b e e w n f
l e p w o i r n a l
y l a d y b i r d y
```

I can find ☐ arthropods.

✓

Explain the difference between vertebrates and invertebrates. ☐ ☐ ☐

Classify animals into different groups. ☐ ☐ ☐

Describe characteristics of different animal groups. ☐ ☐ ☐

Explain what different animals eat. ☐ ☐ ☐

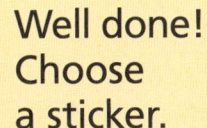

Well done! Choose a sticker.

forty-seven **47**

4 Music land

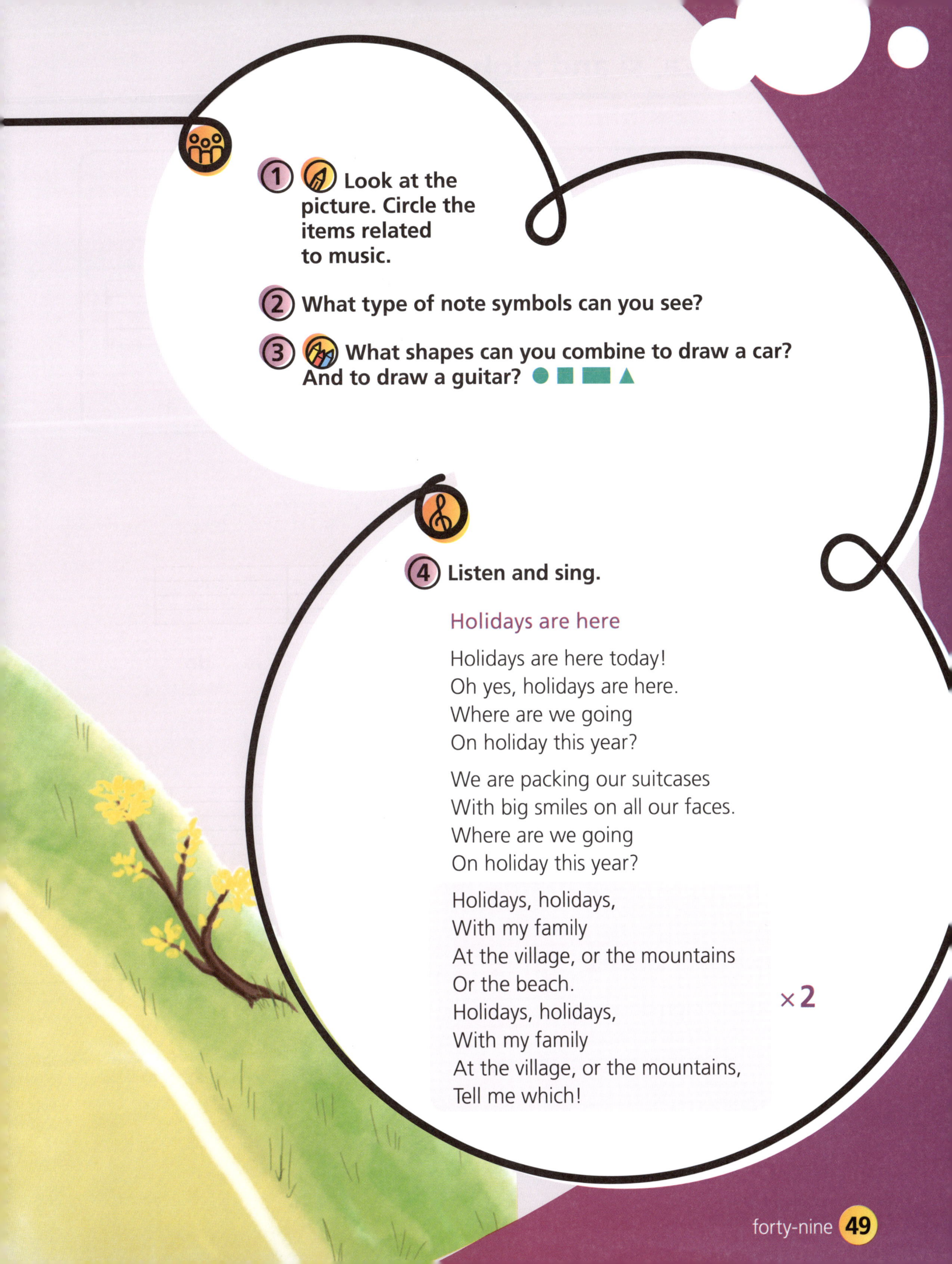

1. Look at the picture. Circle the items related to music.

2. What type of note symbols can you see?

3. What shapes can you combine to draw a car? And to draw a guitar? ● ■ ▬ ▲

4. Listen and sing.

Holidays are here

Holidays are here today!
Oh yes, holidays are here.
Where are we going
On holiday this year?

We are packing our suitcases
With big smiles on all our faces.
Where are we going
On holiday this year?

Holidays, holidays,
With my family
At the village, or the mountains
Or the beach.
Holidays, holidays,
With my family
At the village, or the mountains,
Tell me which!

×2

DISCOVER: La, si and high do

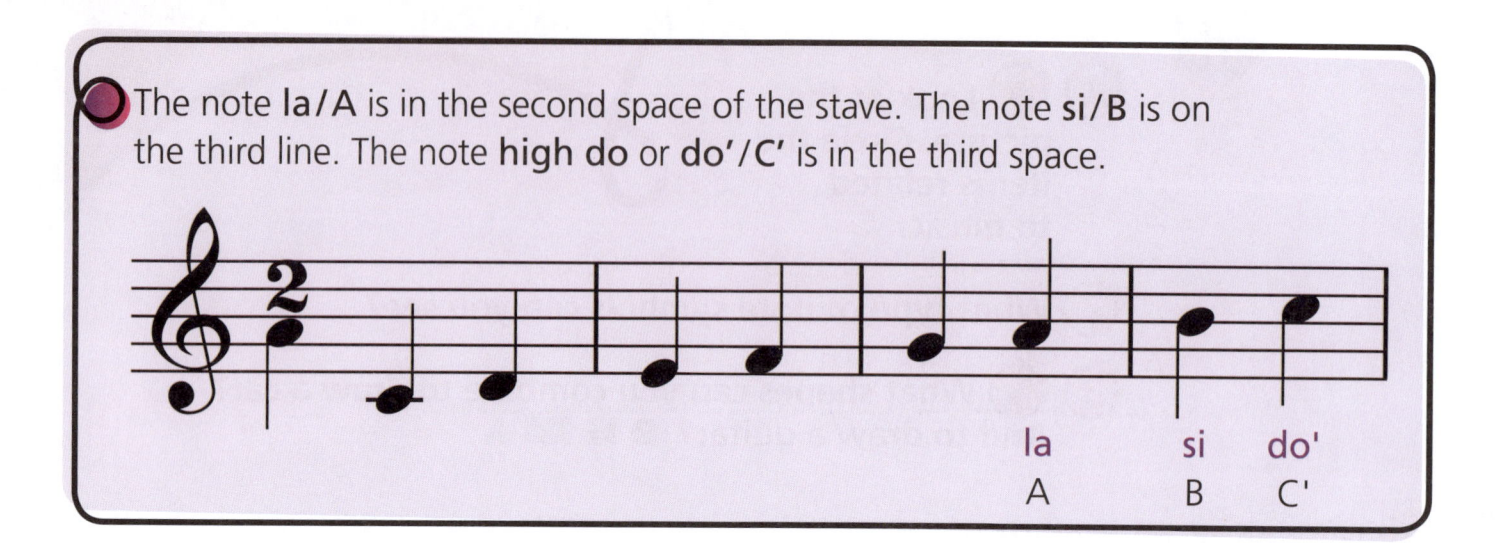

The note **la/A** is in the second space of the stave. The note **si/B** is on the third line. The note **high do** or **do'/C'** is in the third space.

la   si   do'
A   B   C'

1 Write the descending scale on the stave.

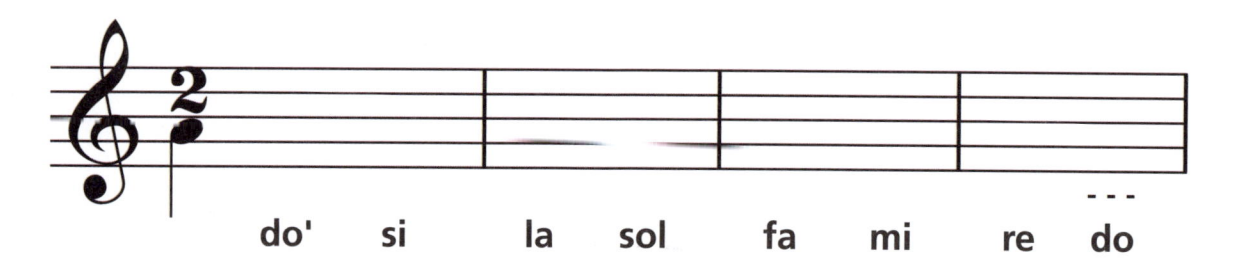

do'   si   la   sol   fa   mi   re   do

2 Complete the stave with the missing crotchets.

E   E   F   G   F   E   D   C

3 Write true (T) or false (F).

A) Notes **do** and **high do** are in a space on the stave. ☐

B) Note **la** is in the third space of the stave. ☐

C) Note **si** is on the third line of the stave. ☐

D) Notes **do** and **do'** are on the same line. ☐

50 fifty

DISCOVER: The world of music

> There are many **professions** related to music.
> - A **composer** composes music.
> - A **musician** plays an instrument.
> - A **luthier** makes and repairs instruments.
> - A **dancer** dances to music.
> - A **conductor** directs musicians in an orchestra.

1 Look and write the professions.

A.

B.

C.

D.

E.

fifty-one 51

LISTEN: Metre

> The **metre** of a piece of music is its rhythmic structure. Composers use different **metres** for different types of music.

1 🔊 **Listen and tap the different metres.**

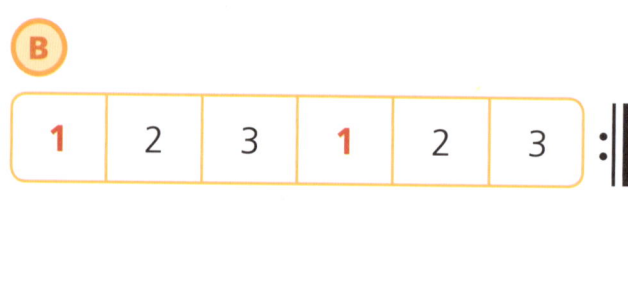

March

A | **1** | 2 | **1** | 2 | **1** | 2 :‖

Waltz

B | **1** | 2 | 3 | **1** | 2 | 3 :‖

52 fifty-two

PLAY: Percussion in a symphony orchestra

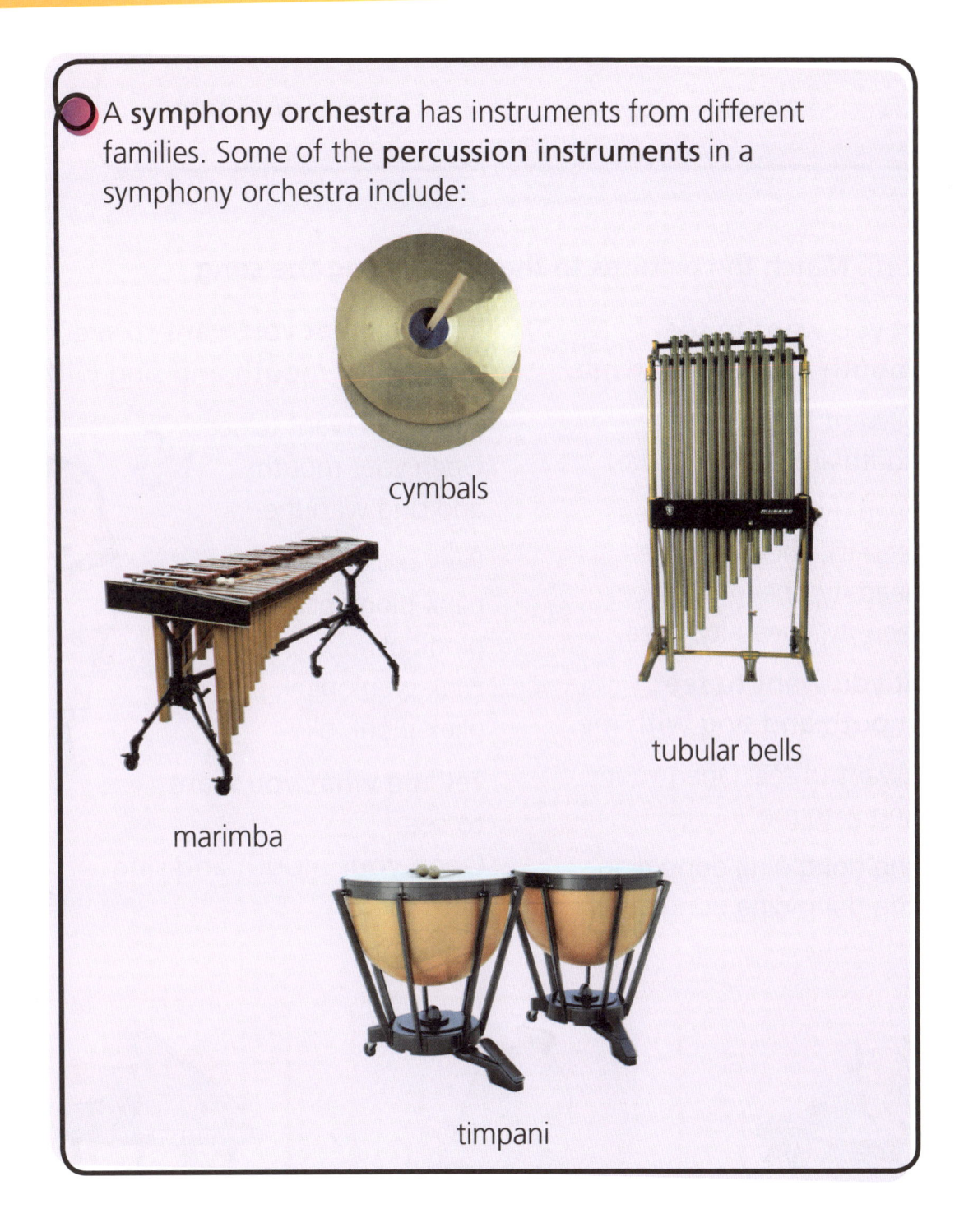

A **symphony orchestra** has instruments from different families. Some of the **percussion instruments** in a symphony orchestra include:

cymbals

tubular bells

marimba

timpani

1 🔊 ✏️ **Listen and write the names of the instruments.**

| sound 1 | sound 2 | sound 3 |

fifty-three **53**

SING: Different voices

> Voices have different qualities, just like musical instruments.

1 🎼 🎨 **Listen. Match the pictures to the voices. Sing the song.**

Tell me what you want to see.
Open your mouth and sing with me.

A small bird, I want to see.
Open your mouth and sing with me.

Cheep-ity, cheep-ity, cheep-ity, chee,
cheep-ity, cheep-ity, cheep-ity, chee.
Cheep-ity, cheep-ity, cheep-ity, chee,
cheep-ity, cheep-ity, cheep-ity, chee.

**Tell me what you want to see.
Open your mouth and sing with me.**

A gold bell, I want to see. Open your mouth and sing with me.

Ding dong ding dong ding dong ding.
Ding dong ding dong ding dong ding.

Tell me what you want to see.
Open your mouth and sing with me.

A piano, I want to see.
Open your mouth and sing with me.

Plink plonk
plink plonk plink
plonk plin.
Plink plonk plink plonk
plink plonk plin.

Tell me what you want to see.
Open your mouth and sing with me.

male voice   female voice   child's voice

CREATE: Form a symphony orchestra

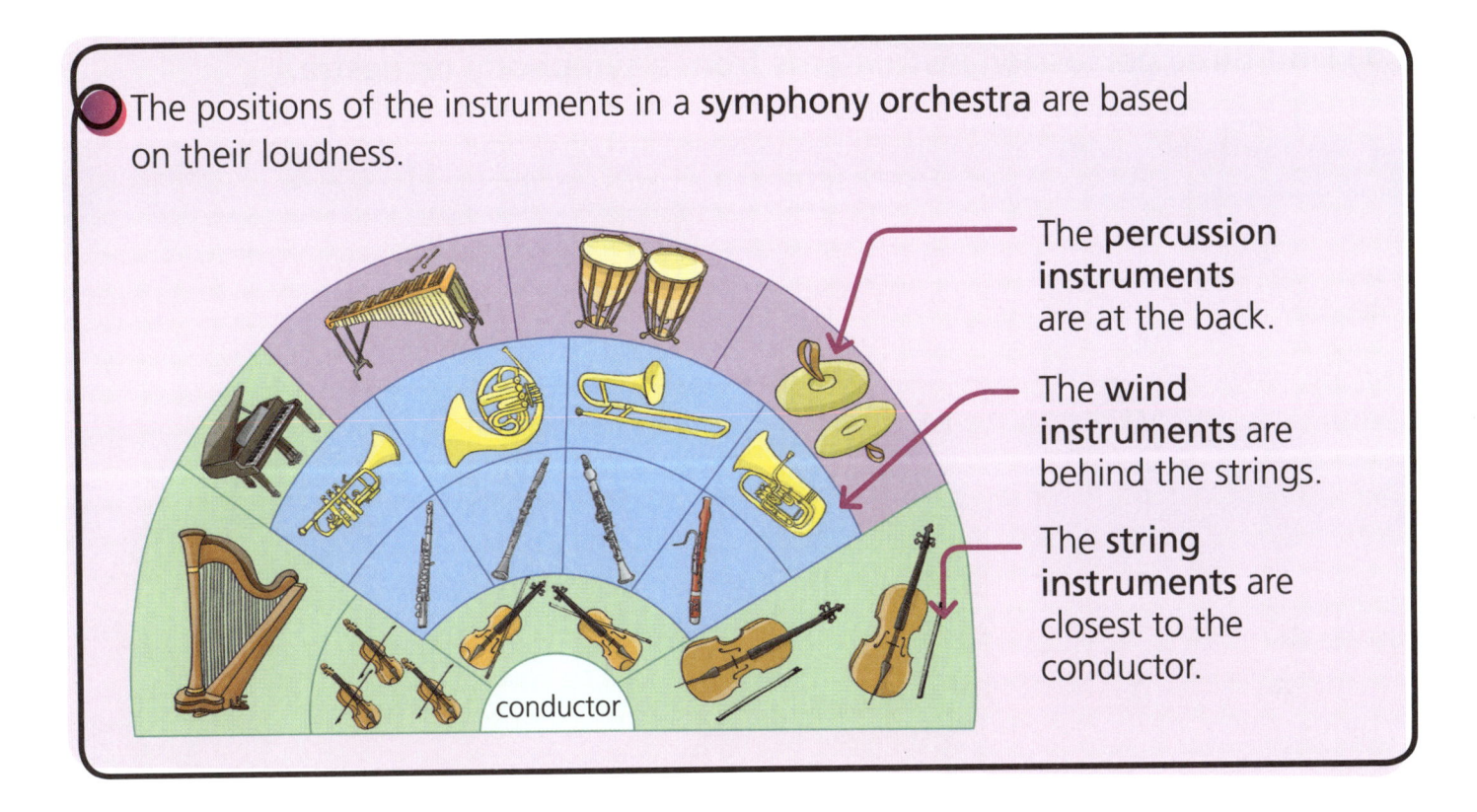

The positions of the instruments in a **symphony orchestra** are based on their loudness.

The **percussion instruments** are at the back.

The **wind instruments** are behind the strings.

The **string instruments** are closest to the conductor.

conductor

Materials

- felt tips or coloured pencils
- scissors
- pencil
- white card

We are going to form an orchestra.

1 **Make three groups.**

Group 1: string instruments

Group 2: wind instruments

Group 3: percussion instruments

2 **Choose an instrument from your group. Draw your instrument on a pieceof card. Cut out your instrument.**

3 **Form the orchestra. Mime playing your instruments.**

fifty-five 55

LET'S REMEMBER

1 Find three percussion instruments from a symphony orchestra.

A	A	X	N	M	P	L	U
T	I	M	P	A	N	I	Q
E	Z	Z	V	R	E	E	E
W	N	M	M	I	O	K	L
R	T	U	P	M	V	B	I
E	C	Y	M	B	A	L	S
C	S	A	C	A	I	L	O

2 Write the notes on the stave.

do' | si | si | la | do' | la | si | do

3 Write the family of each instrument.

_____   _____   _____   _____

4 Talk about your instrument from the symphony orchestra. Describe it to a friend.

- It is *a / an* …

  They are …

- It is a (*percussion / woodwind / brass / string*) instrument.

  They are (*percussion / woodwind / brass / string*) instruments.

- It is made of …

  They are made of …

5 Work in pairs. Take turns as speaker 1 and speaker 2.

Speaker 1		Speaker 2
• A clarinet	is	• a string instrument.
• A violin		• a percussion instrument.
• A flute	isn't	• a woodwind instrument.
• A tuba		• a brass instrument.

Share the sentences with your classmates. Decide if they are true or false.

6 Choose a profession related to music. Play the *yes/no* game with a friend.

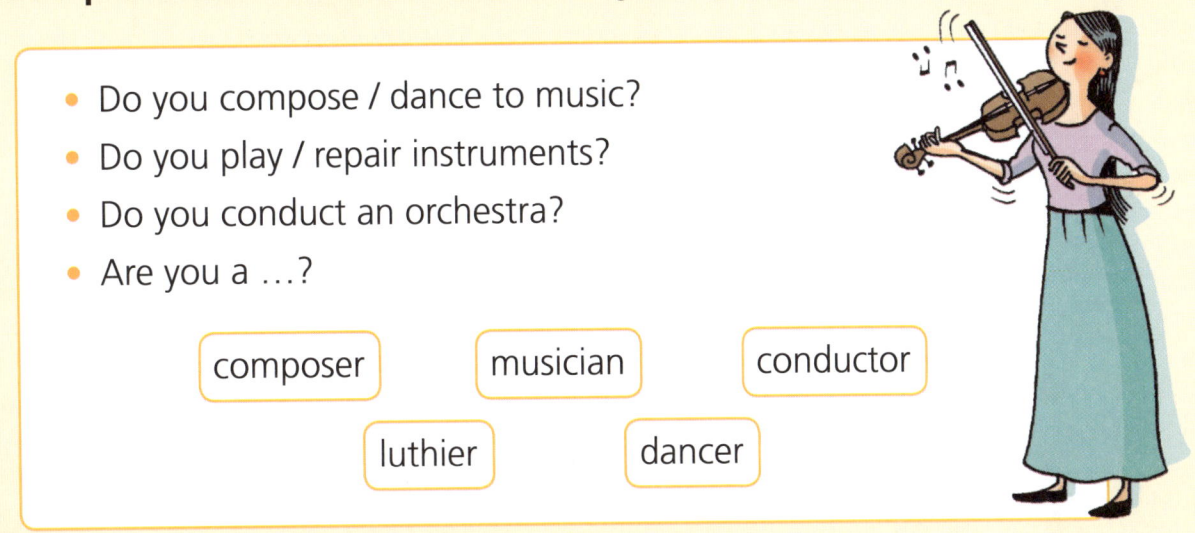

- Do you compose / dance to music?
- Do you play / repair instruments?
- Do you conduct an orchestra?
- Are you a …?

composer   musician   conductor

luthier   dancer

5 The Solar System

1. Find Amy. What is she looking at?

2. What is at the centre of the Solar System?

3. Who is not being a good pupil? Circle.

4. Listen and tick the objects you hear.

Moon   rocket   Sun

telescope   Earth   stars

5. Sing the song and do the actions!

fifty-nine 59

Which planet?

1) 🔊 **Listen, look and point.**

2) ⊕ 🔊 ✏️ **Listen and tick the correct picture.**

What is Sam describing?

sixty

The planets

The **Sun** is a **star** and it is at the centre of the **Solar System**. There are **eight planets** in the Solar System. All the planets move around the Sun. This movement is called **revolution**. What is Amy pointing at?

1 🔊 ✏️ **Listen and label the planets.**

Earth	Venus	Mars	Uranus
Mercury	Neptune	Jupiter	Saturn

2 ✏️ **Tick the correct picture.**

The planets move around the Sun

1 ✏️ **Write the sentences.**

> The Sun is a star.   The Earth is a planet.
> We live on the Earth.   The planets move around the Sun.
> The Sun is at the centre of the Solar System.

○ The Earth takes 365 days, or one year, to complete **one revolution around the Sun**. Mercury, the closest planet to the Sun, takes only 88 days. Look at Sam's chart. How long does it take Neptune to revolve around the Sun?

Saturn	29 years
Uranus	84 years
Neptune	165 years

The Moon moves around the Earth

A **satellite** is an object that moves around a planet or a star. The **Moon** is a satellite because it moves around the Earth. The Sun lights up the Moon, which looks as if it is changing shape. These different shapes are called the **phases** of the Moon.

1 Listen. Find the stickers.

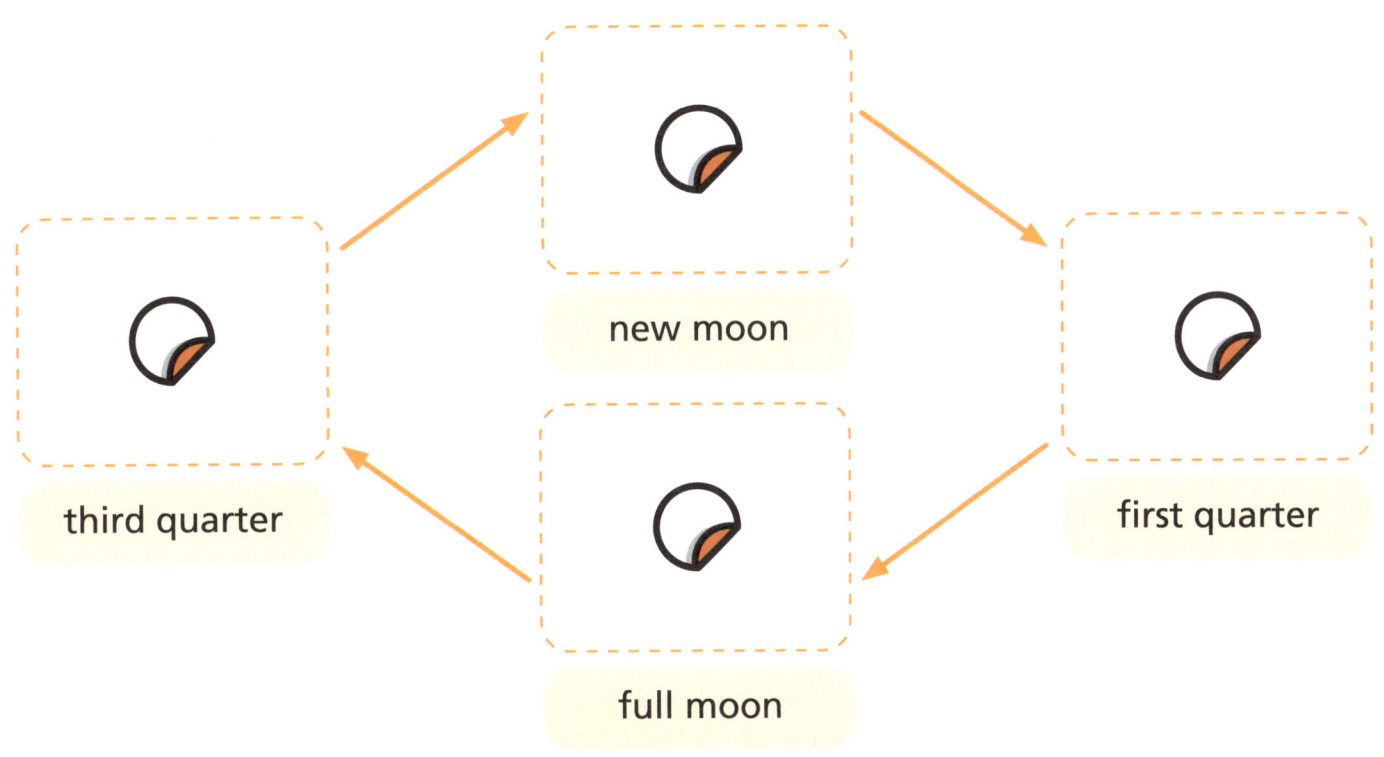

new moon

third quarter

first quarter

full moon

2 Draw the phases of the Moon.

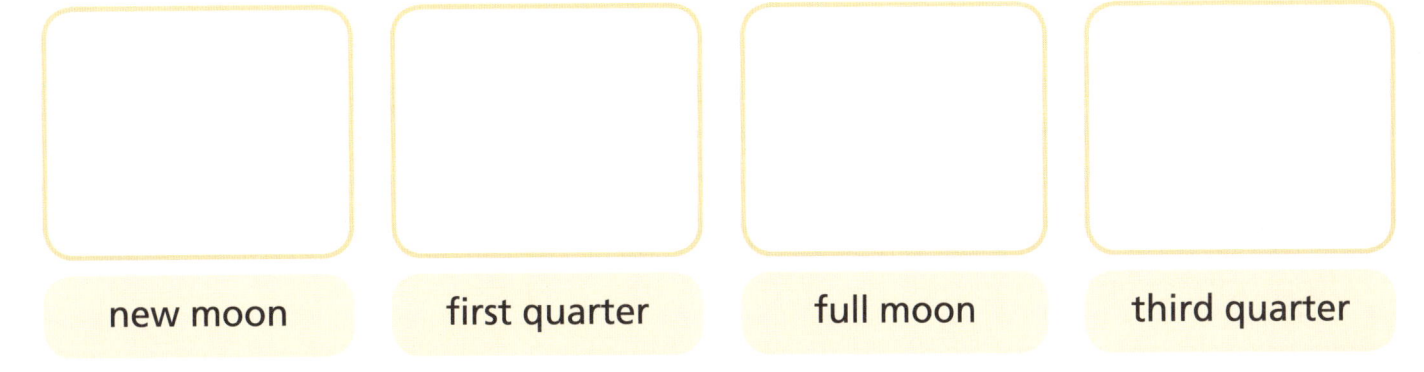

| new moon | first quarter | full moon | third quarter |

Day and night

The Earth is always turning on its axis. This movement is called **rotation** and is the reason we have **day and night**. On the side of the Earth facing the Sun it is day, and on the other side it is night. How long does the Earth take to rotate once?

1 Colour the Earth light and dark. Write *day* and *night*.

2 Listen to the *Time* chant. Write the numbers.

There are _____ hours in one day.
There are _____ minutes in one hour.
A day has _____ parts: morning, afternoon, evening and night.

Seasons and years

1 🔊 ✏️ **Listen and write the seasons.**

autumn   spring   winter   summer

2 ✏️ **Look at the photos and complete the sentences. Write *when it's hot* or *when it's cold*.**

I build a sandcastle _____.

I build a snowman _____.

I wear gloves and a hat _____.

I eat ice cream _____.

○ The Earth takes **one year** to complete **one revolution** around the Sun. There are **twelve months** in a year and **four seasons**: **spring**, **summer**, **autumn** and **winter**. When is Amy's birthday?

sixty-five **65**

LET'S INVESTIGATE: The Sun, Earth and Moon

Project:
Make a model of the Sun, Earth and Moon.

Instructions:

Step 1
Colour and cut out the Sun, Earth and Moon.

Step 2
Cut out two strips of card.

Step 3
Assemble your model and see how everything moves.

1 Circle.

The Earth moves around **the Moon / the Sun**.

The Moon moves around **the Earth / Venus**.

It takes the Earth **24 hours / 365 days** to revolve around the Sun.

It takes the Earth **24 hours / 365 days** to rotate on its axis.

What time is it now? Is it morning or afternoon?

MAKE A DIFFERENCE: Look after your planet

1 🔊 Listen and colour. Use the code.

🟢 good for the environment   🔴 bad for the environment

2 👥 Do a class survey.

❶ Think of questions for your survey.
❷ Ask your classmates.
❸ Draw a chart of your results.

sixty-seven **67**

Let's remember

1. Look and find the words.

```
s a t e l l i t e u
u j k l q w e r h s
n g h c b n j l z t
c p l a n e t d g a
z b n t g i s r g r
a s d f m o o n g s
j e a r t h k l r h
d f g j k i o d g a
a s d f g h j k l q
w e y u j i o f h l
```

2. Label the planets.

3 🖊 **Label the diagram.**

Moon   Earth   Sun   day   night

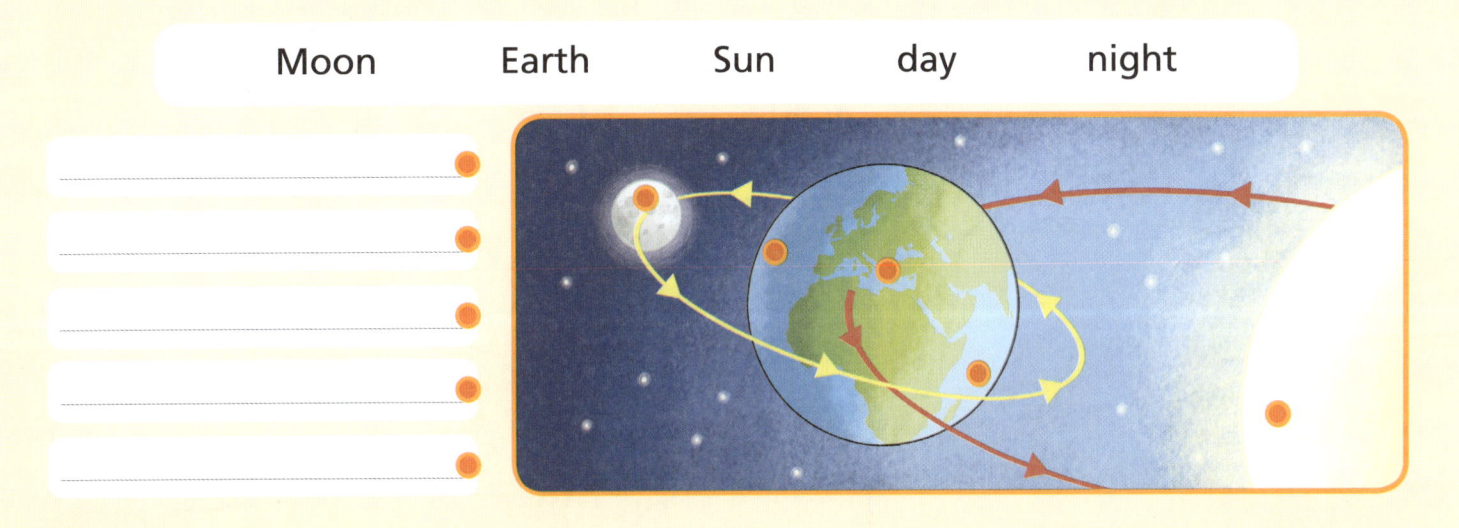

4 🎨 **Draw the phases of the Moon.**

new moon   first quarter   full moon   third quarter

Name the planets in order.

Explain why we have day and night.

Show how the Earth and the Moon move.

Name the seasons.

Well done! Choose a sticker.

# 6 Air and water

1. What is the weather like in the picture?

2. Circle the different weather instruments. Can you name them?

3. Who is not being careful?

4. Listen and number the types of weather in the order you hear them.

stormy foggy rainy

snowy sunny windy

5. Sing the song and do the actions!

seventy-one 71

Measuring the weather

1 🔊 **Listen, look and point.**

2 ✏️ **Look at the pictures. Look at the letters. Write the words.**

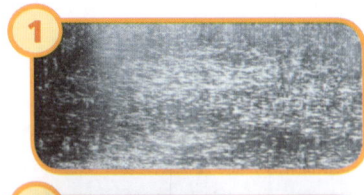

1. Today it is   y i n r a   ....

2. Today it is   n y s n u   ....

3. Today it is   u l c y d o   ....

Wind and clouds

Wind is moving air. A gentle wind is called a **breeze**. A strong wind is called a **gale** and a very strong wind is called a **hurricane**. **Clouds** are made of lots of tiny water droplets. What is Amy pointing at?

1 Write.

hurricane   gale   breeze

2 How are clouds formed? Listen and number.

Precipitation

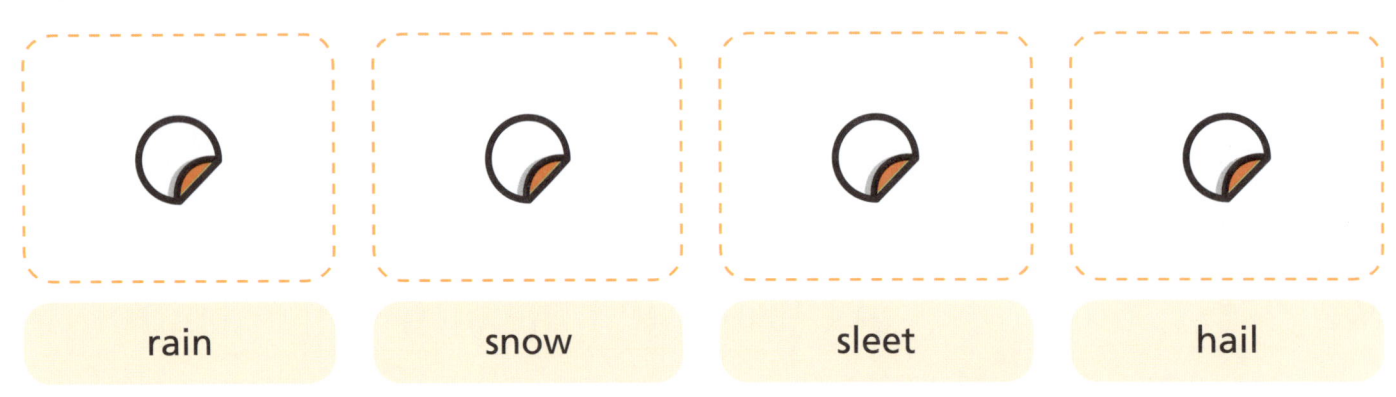

1 🔊 Listen. Find the stickers.

| rain | snow | sleet | hail |

2 🎵 Listen to the *Precipitation* chant. Write.

Precipitation is water that falls from the clouds. It can be liquid or solid. Precipitation normally falls as **rain**, but there are other types of precipitation such as **snow**, **sleet** and **hail**. What are Sam and Amy looking at?

74 seventy-four

What is the weather like today?

1 What is the weather like? Write.

cloudy   foggy   rainy   stormy   sunny
gale   sleet   hail   breeze

2 Record the weather. Draw symbols.

Monday	Tuesday	Wednesday	Thursday	Friday

Weather changes from season to season, but it also changes from day to day. We use **symbols** to represent the different types of weather on a weather map. What symbol is Amy pointing at?

seventy-five

What is air?

Air is all around us. It forms the Earth's **atmosphere**. Air is a mixture of **oxygen** and other gases. All living things need oxygen to live. Air must be clean to keep us healthy. Is Sam breathing clean or dirty air?

1 Tick the things that need oxygen to live.

plants   objects   animals   people   rocks

2 Circle the things that pollute the air we breathe.

What is water?

Water is very important because all living things need water to live. Water changes with heat and cold. In nature we can see water as a **solid**, a **liquid** or a **gas**. What is wrong with Amy's plant?

1 Compare and label the two pictures. Write.

snow ice cloud rain lake river

solid	liquid	gas

2 Investigate. How does water change? Draw the result.

water changes from liquid to gas

water changes from gas to liquid

seventy-seven 77

The water cycle

Water is constantly changing and moving. It is recycled again and again. This process is called the **water cycle**. Look at Sam. What is he standing on? Where does the river go?

1 🔊 ✏️ **Listen and number.**

☐ Water evaporates into the air.

☐ Water falls as rain from the clouds into rivers and lakes.

☐ Water vapour forms clouds.

☐ Water from rivers and lakes flows back into the sea.

2 👥 **Work in pairs. Talk about the water cycle.**

78 seventy-eight

Water around us

Water from the sea is **salt water.** We cannot drink it. We find **fresh water** in rivers and lakes. Before it arrives in our homes, water is cleaned so it can become **drinking water**. Water is important and we must not waste it. Is Amy wasting water?

1 What type of water? Use the code and colour.

salt water ●   fresh water ●   drinking water ●

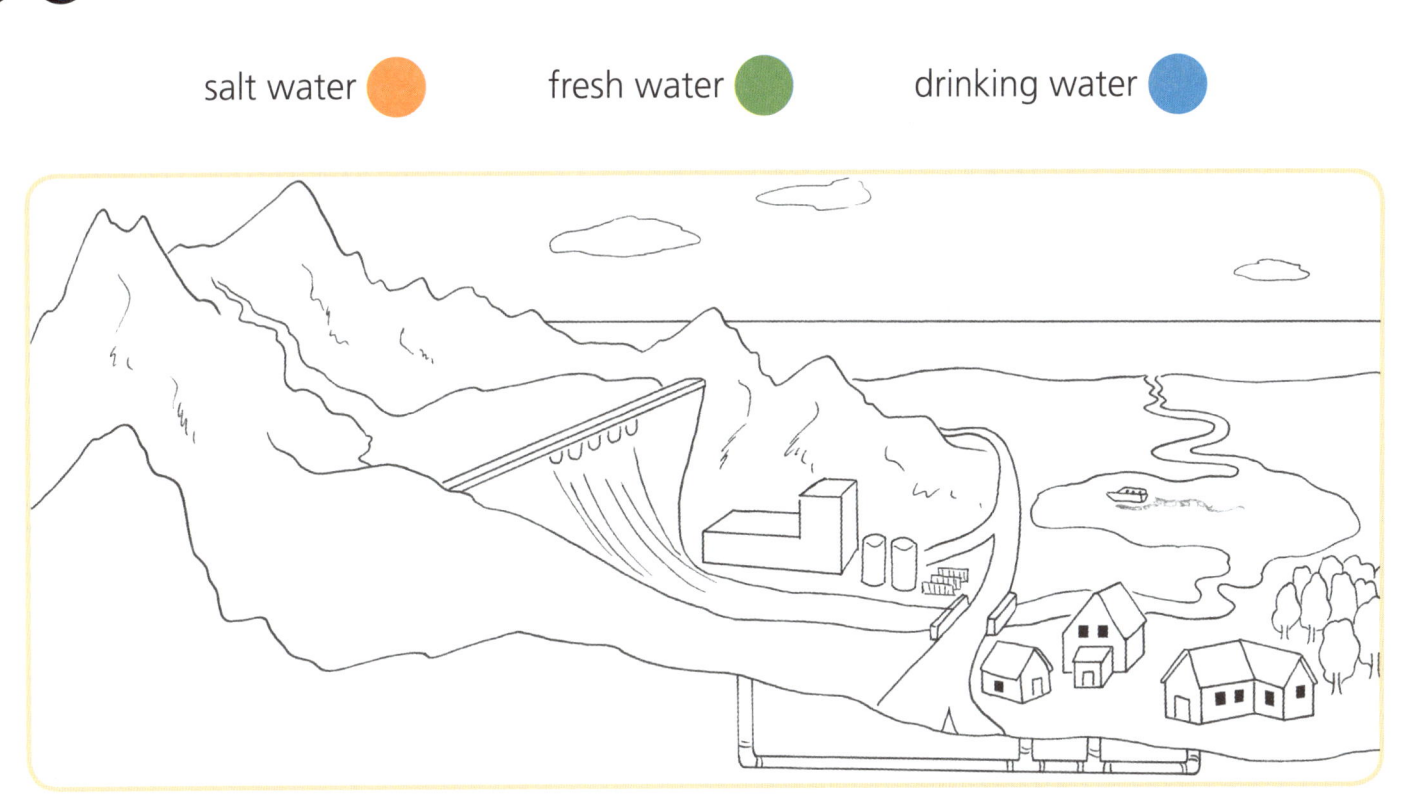

2 How do we use water? Listen and number.

farming    creating electricity    washing    cooking

seventy-nine **79**

LET'S INVESTIGATE: Make a weather vane

Project:

Make a weather vane to investigate the direction of the wind.

Instructions:

Step 1

Decorate and cut out the head and tail of your weather vane.

Step 2

Tape them to both ends of the straw.

Step 3

Attach the straw to the pencil rubber with a pin.

1 Investigate the wind. Write.

- Go outside with your weather vane.
- Your teacher will tell you which direction is north.
- Put the point of your pencil in the centre of the compass.

The wind is blowing from the

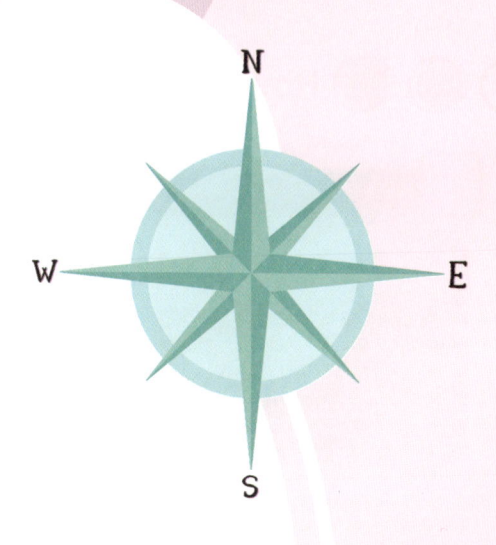

_____.

80 eighty

MAKE A DIFFERENCE: Saving energy

1 🔊 ✏️ How can we save energy? Listen and put a tick or a cross.

2 👥 Protect the planet. Make a *Save energy* leaflet.

① Use books and the internet for ideas.
② Draw pictures and write sentences.
③ Present your leaflet to your classmates.

eighty-one **81**

Let's remember

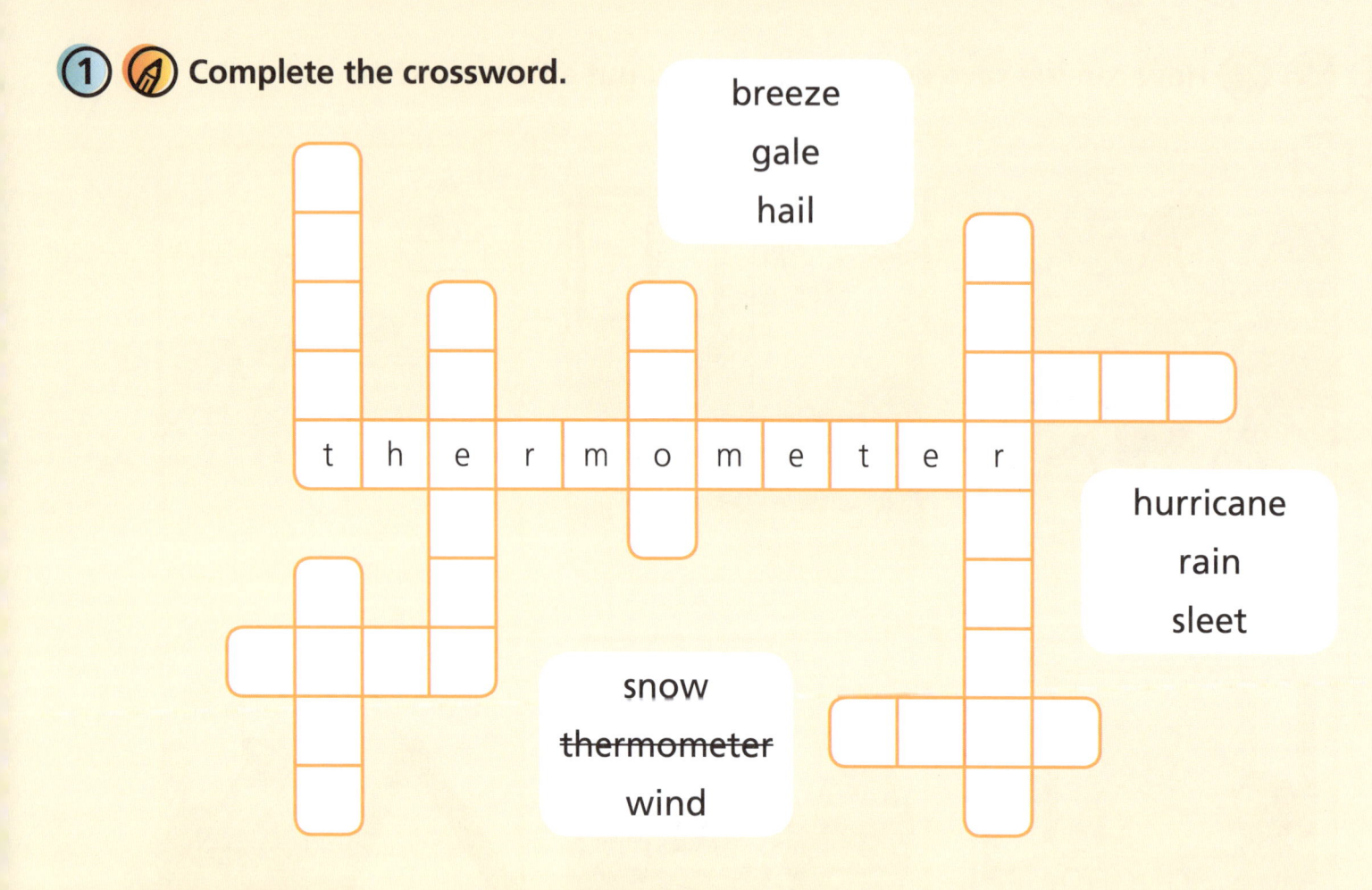

1 **Complete the crossword.**

breeze
gale
hail

t h e r m o m e t e r

hurricane
rain
sleet

snow
~~thermometer~~
wind

2 **What is the weather like? Write.**

_____   _____   _____

_____   _____   _____

82 eighty-two

3. **Match.**

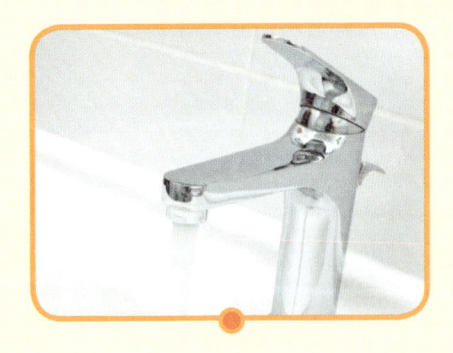

It is drinking water.   It is salt water.   It is fresh water.

4. **Read and number.**

Water flows back to the sea.    Water evaporates.    Water falls from clouds as rain.    Water vapour forms clouds.

Talk about the weather.

Name different types of precipitation.

Describe the water cycle.

Identify salt, fresh and drinking water.

Well done! Choose a sticker.

eighty-three 83

Picture dictionary

1 How my body works

My skeleton

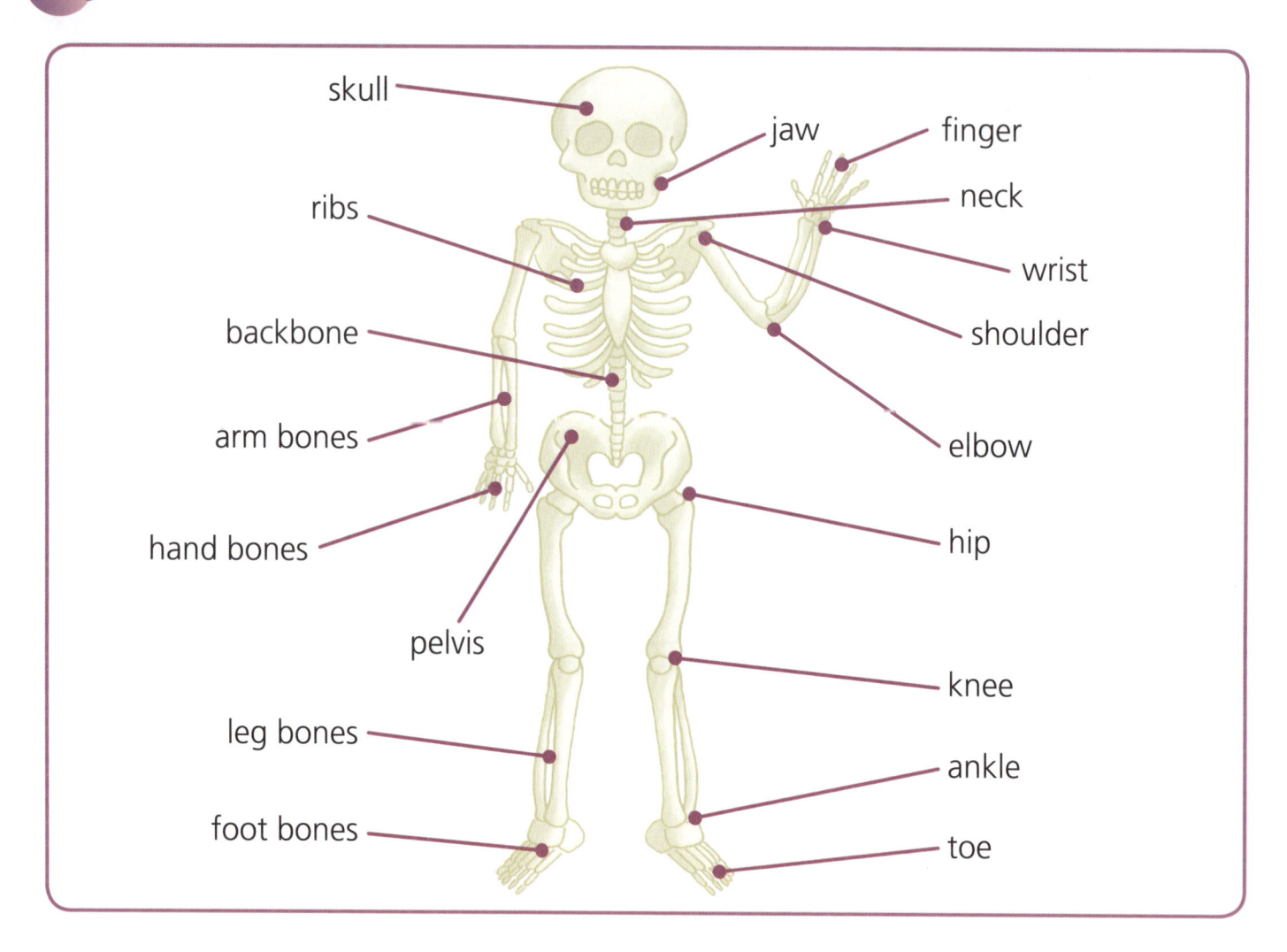

- skull
- jaw
- finger
- ribs
- neck
- backbone
- wrist
- shoulder
- arm bones
- elbow
- hand bones
- hip
- pelvis
- knee
- leg bones
- ankle
- foot bones
- toe

My organs

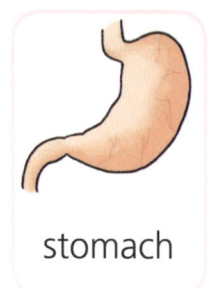

- stomach
- small intestine 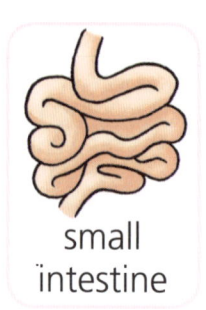
- large intestine 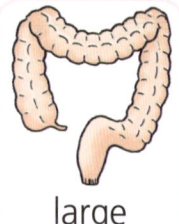
- brain 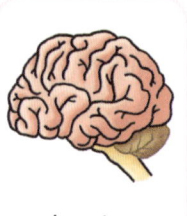
- heart 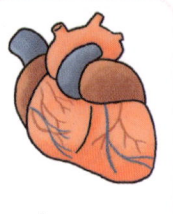
- lungs

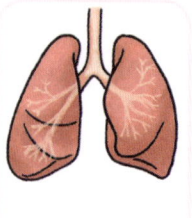

2 Look after yourself

Protect your body

Don't do dangerous activities

Be alert and use your senses

Wear the correct protection

Healthy habits

Eat a balanced diet

Do some exercise

Keep clean

Sleep well

Be a good friend

Play together nicely

Share

Help each other

Picture dictionary

3 The animal kingdom

Vertebrates

mammals — fur

birds — beak, feathers, wings

reptiles — dry skin, scales

amphibians — moist skin

fish — fins, scales, tail, gills

Invertebrates

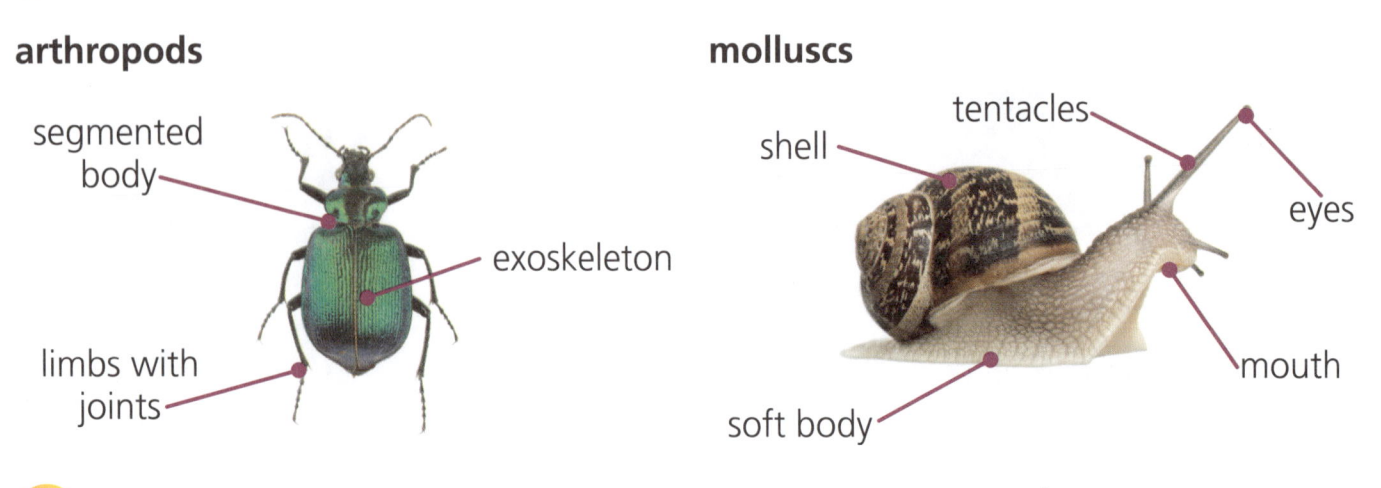

arthropods — segmented body, exoskeleton, limbs with joints

molluscs — shell, tentacles, eyes, mouth, soft body

4 Music Land

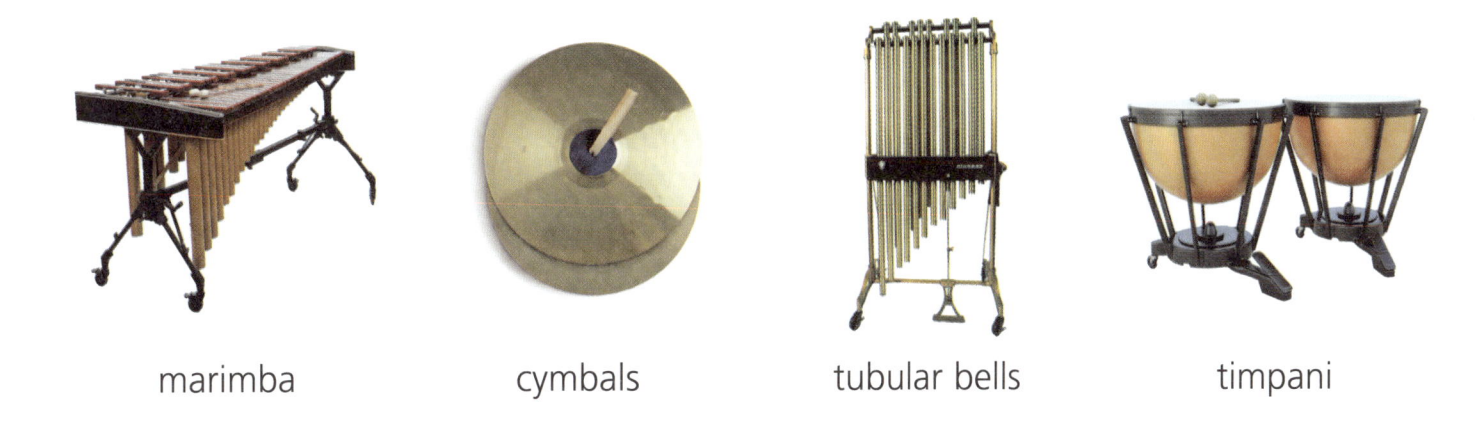

marimba cymbals tubular bells timpani

5 The Solar System

Mercury, Venus, Earth, Mars, Jupiter, Saturn, Uranus, Neptune

Sun Moon stars

Picture dictionary

Phases of the Moon

new moon  | first quarter  | full moon  | third quarter

6 Air and water

Weather

sunny | cloudy | foggy | stormy

hail  | sleet  | breeze  | gale

Unit 1

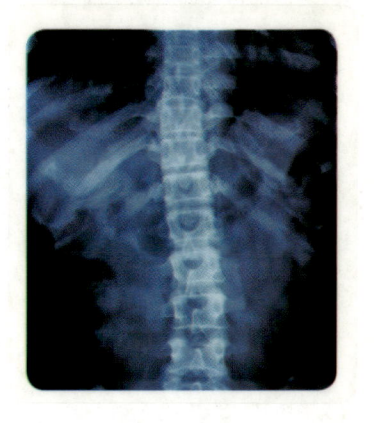

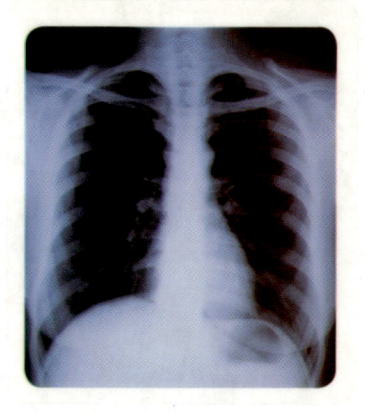

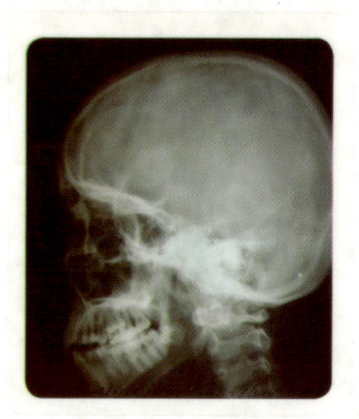

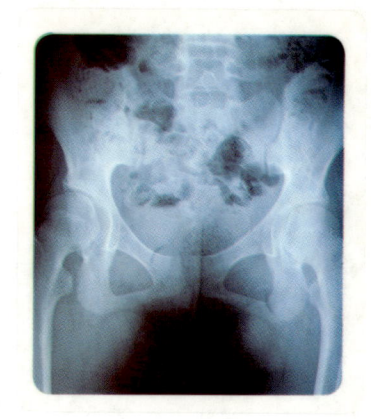

Unit 2

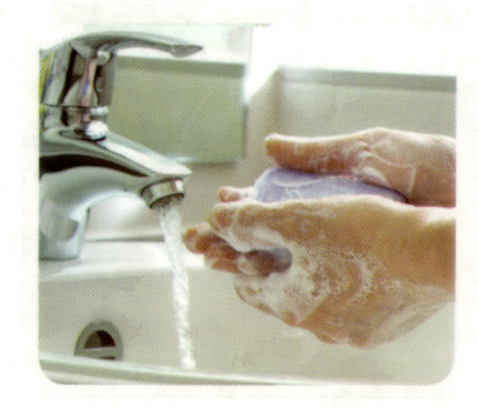

Unit 3

Unit 5

Unit 6